Shakespeare's Sonnets

Blackwell Introductions to Literature

This series sets out to provide concise and stimulating introductions to literary subjects. It offers books on major authors (from John Milton to James Joyce), as well as key periods and movements (from Old English literature to the contemporary). Coverage is also afforded to such specific topics as "Arthurian Romance." All are written by outstanding scholars as texts to inspire newcomers and others: non-specialists wishing to revisit a topic, or general readers. The prospective overall aim is to ground and prepare students and readers of whatever kind in their pursuit of wider reading.

Published

Shakespeare's Sonnets

Dympna Callaghan

Blackwell
Publishing

© 2007 by Dympna Callaghan

BLACKWELL PUBLISHING
350 Main Street, Malden, MA 02148-5020, USA
9600 Garsington Road, Oxford OX4 2DQ, UK
550 Swanston Street, Carlton, Victoria 3053, Australia

The right of Dympna Callaghan to be identified as the Author of this Work has been
asserted in accordance with the UK Copyright, Designs, and Patents Act 1988.

First published 2007 by Blackwell Publishing Ltd

1   2007

Library of Congress Cataloging-in-Publication Data

Callaghan, Dympna.
Shakespeare's sonnets / Dympna Callaghan.
p. cm.—(Blackwell introductions to literature)
Includes bibliographical references and index.
ISBN-13: 978-1-4051-1397-7 (alk. paper)
ISBN-10: 1-4051-1397-9 (alk. paper)
ISBN-13: 978-1-4051-1398-4 (pbk. : alk. paper)
ISBN-10: 1-4051-1398-7 (pbk. : alk. paper)   1. Shakespeare, William,
1564–1616. Sonnets.   2. Sonnets, English—History and criticism.
I. Title.   II. Series.
PR2848.C34 2007
821'.3—dc22
2006022592

A catalogue record for this title is available from the British Library.

Set in 10/13pt Meridian
by SNP Best-set Typesetter Ltd, Hong Kong
Printed and bound in Singapore
by COS Printers Pte Ltd

The publisher's policy is to use permanent paper from mills that operate a
sustainable forestry policy, and which has been manufactured from pulp processed
using acid-free and elementary chlorine-free practices. Furthermore, the publisher
ensures that the text paper and cover board used have met acceptable
environmental accreditation standards.

For further information on
Blackwell Publishing, visit our website:
www.blackwellpublishing.com

For my Father, Edward Callaghan

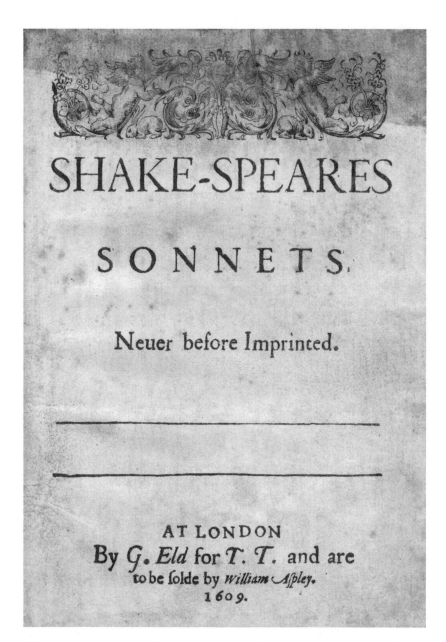

Title page to the first Quarto. Reproduced by permission of the Folger Shakespeare Library.

Contents

Preface

Early in the summer of 1609, while the theatres were closed in the aftermath of an outbreak of plague, *Shakespeare's Sonnets* went on sale for the first time. Published in an easily portable quarto format, measuring five by seven inches, these paper-covered texts were available for sale at the sign of The Parrot in St. Paul's Cross Churchyard, and at Christ Church Gate near Newgate. This slim volume of eighty pages has become one of the greatest works of English poetry. We cannot, alas, recover the precise experience of that moment in the annals of literature, and because extant copies of the first edition of the *Sonnets* are so rare (only thirteen copies survive), fragile and valuable, it is unlikely that most readers will ever see, let alone touch, one of them. For this reason, most readers encounter the sonnets in editions where densely packed critical comments and annotations in small typeface far overwhelm the 154 short poems that Shakespeare wrote. Battered with age and usage, the Quarto itself, in contrast with the scholarly tomes in which most modern editions are presented, is surprisingly unintimidating as a physical object. It contains the sonnets themselves, followed by the long poem, *A Lover's Complaint*, at the end of the book, and otherwise contains no prose matter except for a short dedication page.

The reader's access to the text may be impeded rather than enabled by the barrage of secondary literature that has grown up around *Shakespeare's Sonnets*. Among some of the most controversial of Shakespeare's works, the sonnets have spawned copiously footnoted theories about their composition and about Shakespeare's life that range from plausible scholarly speculation to outrageous invention ungrounded in either historical fact or literary evidence. Such criticism also often ignores the fact that the sonnet is a tightly organized form whose quite rigid parameters serve as the poem's premise: in other words, the pre-existing foundation on which the thought of the sonnet, its ideas, can be expressed. Indeed, much of the energy of Shakespeare's sonnets arises from various degrees of friction and synthesis between form and content, idea and expression, word and image.

The goal of this volume is to provide an introduction to *Shakespeare's Sonnets* rather than to detail new theories about their composition. In deference to their lyrical complexity as well as the passage of time since the sonnets were first published, this volume offers critical guidance as well as analytic insight and illumination. Drawing on key and current critical thinking on the sonnets, the aim of chapters that follow is to engage the poems themselves and to clarify and elucidate the most significant interpretive ideas that have circulated around these complex poems since their first publication.

For all the complexity of the sonnets, whose meanings unfold though layer upon layer of reading and rereading, it is also important to reassure ourselves that they are not beyond normal human understanding. While deeper knowledge of the sonnets will indeed afford a more profound complexity to their meaning, they have been subject to an undue degree of interpretive mystification especially by those who have been looking to decode a hidden meaning about Shakespeare's life. In an endeavor to penetrate the density of Shakespeare's sonnets' structures, ideas, and images, I have provided a brief summary of the central "matter" of each poem at the back of the book. In so doing I have tried to maintain the sense that poetry can never be reduced to or even separated from its rhythms, from the very fact that it *is* verse and therefore an exacerbated act of language, whose intensified resonances and reverberations and variously amplified and compacted meanings make the sonnets such sublime lyrical expressions.

If this book has an agenda it is this: that the focus of the following analysis is on the sonnets rather than on their author. Such a reading is in obedience to Ben Jonson's verse injunction beneath the Droeshout engraving of Shakespeare on the First Folio of 1623 (the first comprehensive edition of Shakespeare's plays), which urges us to read the poet's inventions rather than to invent the poet:

> This figure that thou here seest put,
>   It was not for gentle Shakespeare cut;
>   Wherein the Graver had a strife
>   With Nature, to out-do the life
>   Oh could he but have drawn his wit,
>   As well in brass as he hath hit
>   His face; the print would then surpass
>   All that was ever writ in brass
>   But since he cannot, Reader look
>   Not on his picture, but his book.

While it is impossible to recapitulate the history of the sonnets' reception without recourse to some of the theories that have been expounded over the years, these figure only minimally in the pages that follow. Shakespeare's writing – the poetry itself – is the topic of this volume's assessment.

In order to maintain this focus on the sonnets themselves without undue distraction, I have silently modernized early modern spellings throughout, including those of the Quarto, and kept notes and references to a minimum. Author and title citations to early modern works are given in the text, while the Works Cited list refers to secondary sources.[1] I remain immensely indebted nonetheless to the wealth of scholarly and editorial labor that has gone before me.

CHAPTER 1

Introduction: Shakespeare's "Perfectly Wild" Sonnets

> He had at last discovered the true secret of Shakespeare's Sonnets; that all the scholars and critics had been entirely on the wrong track, and that he was the first, who, working purely by internal evidence, had found out who Mr. W. H. really was. He was perfectly wild with delight.
>
> Oscar Wilde, *Portrait of Mr. W. H.* (1889)

In Oscar Wilde's story, *Portrait of Mr. W. H.*, the narrator's friend, Cyril Graham, purports to have discovered the "secret" of the sonnets. This great secret of the sonnets is, of course, the identity of the young man to whom most of the sonnets were written. Cyril's theory and indeed Cyril himself, whose obsession with the identity of the young man precipitates his descent into madness and suicide, turn out to be like Wilde's onomastic pun "perfectly wild." The theory is, in other words, simultaneously lunatic and the epitome of the author's own transgressive homoerotic posture amid the straight-laced hypocrisies of English Victorian culture. (Wilde was tried, convicted, and imprisoned for sodomy.) Wilde's novella neatly summarizes a range of theories on the sonnets while also wittily demonstrating them to be what one of the great critics of these poems, Stephen Booth, has described as the "madness" they seem to induce: "[T]hese sonnets can easily become what their critical history has shown them to be, guide posts for a reader's journey into madness" (Booth, 1977, x). Indeed, Wilde's character Cyril Graham ends up committing suicide on the continent; but by then the contagion of his obsession has also infected the hitherto skeptical narrator of the story.

So what is the mystery of the sonnets, and what provokes generation after generation of readers with the urge to solve it? *Shakespeare's Sonnets* is a series – and arguably a sequence (a deliberate narrative arrangement of poems) – of 154 poems, which refer to three principal characters: first, the poet himself, the "I," the speaker of the *Sonnets* whose thoughts and feelings they relate. This "I" may be a direct representation of Shakespeare himself or a more mediated figure, namely the persona of the poet, who plays the role named "I" throughout the course of the poems. The title of the volume, *Shakes-peare's Sonnets*, however, actively encourages the reader to identify Shakespeare with the voice of the sonnets. This point is reinforced by the fact that Thomas Heywood refers to Shakespeare as publishing his sonnets "in his own name" (Duncan-Jones, 1997, 86). Stephen Greenblatt observes that "Many love poets of the period used a witty alias as a mask: Philip Sidney called himself 'Astrophil'; [Edmund] Spenser was the shepherd 'Colin Clout'; Walter Ralegh (whose first name was pronounced 'water'), 'Ocean.' But there is no mask here; these are as the title announces, *Shakes-peare's Sonnets*" (Greenblatt, 233).

The second character in the sonnets is the addressee of the first 126 poems, a fair young man, the "fair friend" (Sonnet 104), or a "lovely boy" as the poet calls him in Sonnet 126. It is typically assumed that the sonnets refer to a single male addressee rather than to different young men. Similarly, the remainder of the poems, Sonnets 127–154, are understood to be mainly about a single "woman colored ill." She has come to be known as the "dark lady," even though Shakespeare himself never calls her that. The poems do not name any of these figures even though there are a number of poems (135, 136, and 143) that pun on the name "Will," which is of course an abbreviation of "William," Shakespeare's own name. But since William is such a common name, it is also not beyond the realm of possibility that "Will" is also the name of the youth.

Other sonnet sequences, even when plainly composed more of fiction than fact, name their addressees: Shakespeare's famous Italian predecessors give their sonnet characters names: Dante writes to Beatrice; Petrarch's *Canzoniere* addresses his beloved Laura; and there is no secrecy surrounding the identity of Tommaso Cavalieri, the real-life figure to whom the great artist Michelangelo addressed many of his sonnets. Among Shakespeare's contemporaries, Thomas Lodge's eponymous sequence names the object of its devotion in the title:

Phillis (1593), as does Samuel Daniel's *Delia* (1592), while Richard Barnfield's *Cynthia* (1595) contains amorous sonnets written to a male addressee, Ganymede, the mythological name for Jove's cup-bearer. Shakespeare's great English predecessor in the sonnet form, Sir Philip Sidney, puns on his own name, Philip, in the title of his sequence of 118 poems, *Astrophil and Stella*. "Astrophil" means star lover, while "Stella," as well as being a first name, is the Latin word for star. Sidney's sonnet sequence, however, unlike *Shakespeare's Sonnets*, reveals the lady's real historical identity as that of Lady Penelope Rich. The absence of specificity in Shakespeare is, furthermore, not just about names, but also about times and places. Whereas in Petrarch, for example, who was the most important precursor of all European sonnet writing, we are told the day and exact time the poet met Laura, April 6, 1327, at the Church of St. Clare in Avignon; or to take an example temporally closer to Shakespeare, Samuel Daniel tells us of his trip to Italy. In Shakespeare's sonnets in contrast, we never find out when or where, let alone why or how, the poet, the "lovely boy," and the "woman colored ill" met. We are given only the broadest hints: Sonnet 107 suggests the poet met the youth three years previously; 77 and 122 refer to the gift of a notebook from the poet to the youth; 50 and 110 describe journeys that separate the poet and the youth. The combination of such tantalizing hints and the absence of specific information is partly what has fueled an inferno of speculation over the centuries. What makes readers desperate to know "the real story," the back-story or the secret of these poems, is not just that the poet in Shakespeare's sonnets seems so emotionally invested in both the figures he writes about (that is true of many poets), or even that the poet intimates a specifically erotic interest in the youth he writes about (Michelangelo and Barnfield, as we have seen, also did that), but that the poet appears to be caught in a painful love triangle with the youth and the woman, whom he accuses of seducing his "fair friend." In other words, there is a singularly scandalous scenario at the heart of what is unquestionably one of the greatest aesthetic achievements in the English language.

It is in part this scandal, or to be more accurate this complex constellation of relationships between the three principal characters and the degree of emotional reality with which they are rendered, that makes it impossible to regard the sonnets as entirely fictional, at least in any simple or straightforward sense. An important constituent of the aesthetic achievement of these poems is that the "Two loves" (Sonnet 144) are so vividly realized, but with only the barest recourse to external reality: the man is fair, the woman dark; he is beautiful, she not, or if she is, it is a beauty that defies conventional definition. This is the entirety of concrete description that we possess. We could not pick out these people from a police line-up, and yet we have intimate knowledge of the rapture and turbulence they have provoked within the emotional and psychic life of the poet. This is, of course, because in lyric we are not given a portrait of the individual to whom the poem is addressed. Rather, we are shown the contours of a deep impression made by the individual on the mind of the poet. This is the very nature and essence of a lyric image – that is, it is the poetic (mental and emotional) impression of real people and real events, without ever aspiring to the status of a record or description of the people and events themselves. This is an important though subtle distinction occupying neither the terrain of history nor that of fiction, but precisely the landscape of the irreducibly literary imagination. We will return to this conundrum many times in the course of this book – that is, to the fact that as readers, we are privy to the most intimate knowledge about the poet's feelings and relationships, without knowing the slightest thing about the empirical facts and circumstances related to them.

This mystery of identity is not only contained within actual sonnets themselves, but is also announced on the notoriously cryptic dedication page of the first edition of *Shakespeare's Sonnets*, the 1609 Quarto, which famously reads:

TO. THE. ONLIE. BEGETTER. OF
THESE. INSVING. SONNETS.
Mr. W.H. ALL. HAPPINESE.
AND. THAT. ETERNITIE.
PROMISED.
BY.
OVR.EVER-LIVING POET.
WISHETH.
THE WELL-WISHING.
ADVENTURER. IN
SETTING.
FORTH.
T. T.

This is the "Mr. W. H." of the title of Oscar Wilde's story, and indeed like Wilde's character, Cyril Graham, many readers have taken Mr. W. H. to be one and the same as the fair youth addressed in the poems. The one thing we do know about this dedication is that the initials beneath it are those of Thomas Thorpe, the publisher. The title-page informs the reader that the volume was printed "By G. Eld for T. T." Here, "for" means "on behalf of," and Thorpe's name was entered into the Stationers' Register (the official record of all books that were licensed for print publication) as possessing the license to print, on May 20, 1609.

Whatever the identity of the elusive W. H. (a question we will address later in this book), that the dedication is, literally at any rate, Thorpe's rather than Shakespeare's is reinforced by Thorpe's reverential reference to Shakespeare as "our ever-living poet." But what does it mean that W. H. is the "begetter" ("father" or "progenitor") of the sonnets? Potentially, he is their patron and/or their inspiration, but would that be the inspiration for Thomas Thorpe to publish them or for William Shakespeare to write them? Whoever Mr. W. H. is, Thorpe wishes him the everlasting renown that Shakespeare promises the young man in the poems themselves. Indeed, that only initials allude to the identity of the dedicatee links him with the unnamed youth of the poems. Further, it is reasonable to assume that W. H. and the fair friend are one and the same because Thorpe, who took it upon himself to commit *Shakespeare's Sonnets* to print, is also one of the first readers of the 1609 Quarto (possibly even the first reader, since even the youth or the lady, if they really exist, might not have been privy to the whole contents of the volume), a fact that we know because his dedication reveals that he has already read the poems and knows that they promise eternal fame to the young man. Thorpe and the poet are privy to the identity of the fair youth and know whether or not he is rendered "to the life" or as a fictional character in those poems that refer to him. Thorpe's dedication reveals a sense of the joint enterprise between himself and "our ever-living poet" and possibly the shared hope of receiving financial reward upon their publication. It is in this sense that Thorpe the publisher is "the well-wishing adventurer," the well-meaning, well-intentioned entrepreneur who has taken upon himself the risk of publication. He sends Mr. W. H. good wishes "in setting forth," at the outset of the enterprise, the beginning of the book. This at least is the syntactic logic of the dedication, though some readers have taken "the well-wishing adventurer" to refer not to Thorpe but to the young man whom it is assumed is about to set forth on some voyage. That the dedicatee of the volume is not named has enticed readers to play with the dedication (as indeed they have done with the poems themselves) as if it were an encryption and that the normal rules of sentence structure should be assumed not to apply. This is often the first step in the direction of the madness that Stephen Booth felt the sonnets stimulated in all too many readers.

Wilde's fictional character Cyril Graham is adamant about the foundation of the sonnets in Shakespeare's actual experience: "Still less would he admit that they were merely a philosophical allegory, and that in them Shakespeare is addressing his Ideal Self, or Ideal Manhood, or the Spirit of Beauty, or Reason, or the Divine Logos, or the Catholic Church. He felt, as indeed I think we all must feel, that the sonnets are addressed to an individual – to a particular young man whose personality for some reason seems to have filled the soul of Shakespeare with terrible joy, and no less terrible despair" (Wilde, 29–30). The sonnets do indeed bespeak a powerful emotional reality, one that might indeed be illuminated by the discovery of some hitherto unknown historical fact – such as the identity of the "boy" or the "woman" – but probably not one that will "solve" or explain them once and for all. The sonnets are neither biographical encryptions nor word puzzles to be deciphered even by the sophisticated technical vocabularies of prosody and rhetoric. The tantalizing dearth of information in the sonnets marks a fundamentally different order of reality, a profoundly lyrical and irreducibly literary way of representing not external reality but the perceptions of someone who looks at the world from the inside out (see Schoenfeldt, 320). From this vantage point, from within, the poetic imagination is applied to relationships, and not merely as self-expression but as a very carefully crafted series of ideas held within the tension of the sonnet form.

With the exception of a brief excerpt from a play penned by multiple authors, *Sir Thomas More* (ca. 1595), which constitutes the longest surviving sample of Shakespeare's handwriting, we do not have any autograph manuscripts of Shakespeare's works, including the sonnets. Manuscript versions of the sonnets are, however, mentioned in 1598 in a book called *Palladis Tamia: Wits Treasury*, written by the Cambridge schoolmaster and cleric Francis Meres. He writes of the circulation of Shakespeare's "sugared sonnets among his private friends," which offers a clue to their manuscript publication long before their appearance in print, and also gives us some hint about the date of composition. Two sonnets (138 and 144) were printed in a volume of poetry called *The Passionate Pilgrim* in 1599, and all 154 poems, together with a longer poem called *A Lover's Complaint*, were published in the Quarto edition of 1609.

These snippets of information lead us to some key issues. First, we know from Meres's remark that Shakespeare must have begun working on the sonnets over a decade *before* they saw print, and he is believed to have begun writing sonnets around 1590. It is important to remember that as a genre, poetry in general and sonnets in particular were not necessarily composed with the aim of print publication in view. Further, while we regard publication (making writing public) as synonymous with print, this was not the case in early modern England, where *manuscript* or *scribal publication* thrived alongside print publication. Thus writers "published" in manuscript, that is, "made public" handwritten copies of poems. This form of publication relied on hand-to-hand circulation as well as the laborious process of copying with a quill and ink from the author's manuscript. There were hundreds of professional scribes in London, literate people, usually men, who made copies for a living. For centuries, around St. Paul's Cathedral, small armies of literate clergy engaged in the clerical work connected with ecclesiastical registers, ledgers and church records, and the like. Indeed, it is this history that led to the centering of the London book trade in Shakespeare's time around St. Paul's Cathedral and to the preponderance of booksellers that grew up around it in that area. The Quarto of the sonnets could be purchased at two locations in London, one of which was the shop of William Aspley at the sign of The Parrot in St. Paul's Cross Churchyard, and the other was at the premises of the bookseller William Wright at Christ Church Gate near Newgate. While the publication history of the Quarto is important, then, the history of the sonnets themselves begins in the complex web of manuscript rather than print publication.

Although the book trade was focused around St. Paul's in Shakespeare's London, the vast energies applied to administrative labors of scribes and clerks took place more than anywhere else in the service of the exponentially expanding legal system. Scribes connected with the complex legal apparatuses of the courts and the crown copied out primarily legal documents, such as deeds, wills, dowry agreements, parliamentary records, and sovereign decrees. It is no accident, therefore, that there was a concentration of such persons around the Inns of Court, the center of legal training in England. This was also where poetry flourished, as literate young men applied their wit to various forms of verse. Indeed, Shakespeare's plays had been performed in this setting and his own knowledge of the legal profession is amply demonstrated in the sonnets.

However, copying was not just a professional activity. Commonplace or table books (a kind of early modern journal) flourished in environments of educated young men. In these blank books, poems, jokes, and biblical quotations were transcribed, and many of Shakespeare's sonnets are to be found in commonplace books compiled after their 1609 publication (see Roberts, 10). That people copied out their favorite Shakespeare sonnets not only demonstrates their early popularity, but also once again emphasizes the fact that a significant manuscript culture persisted, and even flourished, throughout the seventeenth century directly alongside an increasingly pervasive culture of print.

Necessarily of course, scribal publication reached a far more limited audience than that of print, but for some poets this was positively advantageous. For example, Shakespeare's illustrious predecessor in the sonnet form, Sir Philip Sidney, would hardly have wanted "the stigma of print" attached to a sonnet sequence that treated his adulterous longings for the married Penelope Rich. However, it was not the capacity for personal revelation that constituted the greatest impediment to printing sonnets but, rather, the environment of a post-Reformation Puritanism that was ideologically predisposed to regard poetry as at best a frivolous pastime, and at worst a force of moral degradation. In fact, the sonnet form was fundamentally aristocratic, written until well into the sixteenth century by people associated with the royal court, people whose primary identity was that of courtier or statesman rather than professional writer. While courtiers and statesmen might well be poets, and sonnet writing in particular was an art cultivated amongst the elite, they did not depend upon writing for their livelihood. Not so with Shakespeare: he was a professional who wrote for money, primarily dramatic verse, which was in the first instance performed on stage rather than published in print. But that he entered into the arena of scribal publication, as Meres's remark suggests, indicates that in writing the sonnets he followed the path more typical of his sonneteering social superiors. Also, there is no indication that this means of circulation was employed in relation to any of Shakespeare's other poems, even to *The Lover's Complaint*, which is appended to the 1609 *Sonnets*. On the contrary, the title-pages of Shakespeare's two long narrative poems or epyllia, *Venus and Adonis* and *The Rape of Lucrece*, are clear that they were both written for Shakespeare's patron, Henry Wriothesley, Earl of Southampton. Similarly, *The Phoenix and the Turtle*, Shakespeare's riddling contribution to a volume called *Love's Martyr* (1601), was written for very specific circumstances as part of a volume put together by Robert Chester to commemorate the knighthood of Sir John Salusbury.

Of course, we do not know precisely how widely Shakespeare's manuscript sonnets were circulated. We do know that they were sufficiently known in this form for Meres to remark on it *in print* in a book about the major literary achievements of the English language. However, it is also the case that commonplace books that survive from the 1590s show no evidence that Shakespeare's sonnets were in circulation, which suggests that the "private friends" constituted a deliberately restricted circle of readers but that the circulation was not so small that it was only of the order of sharing the poems with a couple of trusted confidants as a kind of vetting mechanism prior to publication.

Unfortunately, we do not know which of Shakespeare's sonnets were circulated this way. Certainly, those published in *The Passionate Pilgrim* in 1599 – presenting the "dark lady" as a liar and a whore – do not easily conform to the adjective "sugared." Nor do we know who transcribed the sonnets Meres saw, but the very fact that the sonnets achieved manuscript publication before print publication indicates that Shakespeare had entered into one of the most common ways of accessing a readership for verse in this period. In this scribal method of publication, too, different versions of a poem might be in circulation at one time, and sometimes deliberately or unwittingly, the original poem might be altered in the process of making the copy. For an author who was concerned that his poem was accurately transcribed there were decided advantages to print publication. One conspicuous advantage was that once the type was set, all subsequent copies were the same, despite the fact that there was a certain latitude in the typesetting process, where a compositor might insert capitals where the author had not placed them, or who might, given the vagaries of early modern spelling, spell a word differently (or indeed even in several different ways) than it was spelled in the manuscript page he was copying from. There existed a very generous margin of human error in the Elizabethan printing house between the way the words appeared on the author's handwritten (and sometimes hard to decipher) manuscript and the process of getting them on to the page as print. Every single letter of every single word had to be set line by line by the compositor in an enormously labor-intensive process of setting movable metal type. Compositors often attached the page of the manuscript they were working on to an object known as a *visorum*, a kind of stand that allowed the compositor to look up at the manuscript as he worked and thus facilitated the hand–eye coordination involved in setting the type. All too often, however, the compositor's eye was quicker than his hand, so that the printed text, far from being a direct and accurate transcription of the author's words, might be a significantly different version of what originally appeared in the manuscript copy.

Was the fact that in Shakespeare's Sonnet 1, for example, the word rose, which appears in the middle of a line, is both capitalized like a proper name and italicized as *"Rose"* a deliberate decision on Shakespeare's part, or merely the result of the vagaries of the printing process? In truth, we do not know. Or, is the visually alliterative image in Sonnet 6, "winter's wragged hand," an integral part of the poem as Shakespeare wrote it? Or is it just an archaic spelling, harking back to a time when "ragged" was probably pronounced, as it still is in Cockney English, more like "wragged," something that we need not concern ourselves with because we do not know for certain that the prefatory "w" in "wragged" is Shakespeare's rather than the printer's? Notably, modernized editions of the *Sonnets* must do away not only with this particular "w" but also with vast dimensions of the poems, changing rhymes, pronunciations, homonyms – the sound of the poems and the impact of the sonnet itself as an "image" on the page.

A modernized version of the poem is, in essence, a different poem. Arguably, too, we cannot refuse to concern ourselves with the poems exactly as they appear in the 1609 Quarto, simply because while we do not know for certain that they are printed there exactly as Shakespeare conceived them, it is similarly true that we do not know the reverse to be the case. That this is an issue at all is testimony to the difference between early modern printing practices and our own. Though there were conventions about authorship and the idea that a given work "belonged" in some sense to the person who wrote it, the early modern period did not possess anything so clearly codified as modern laws about an author's copyright (see Erne, 2–10). There are several instances in this period of works that were printed without the permission or even the knowledge of their authors, a circumstance which authors might complain about but could do nothing to remedy. A very pertinent example of this phenomenon is the unauthorized collection of poems whose title-page reads *The Passionate Pilgrim by W. Shakespeare* printed in 1599 by William Jaggard. In fact, there are only two of the *Sonnets*, "When My Love Swears That She is Made of Truth" (Sonnet 138 is the revised version in the Quarto) and "Two Loves Have I of comfort and despair" (Sonnet 144 in the Quarto), and three further poems by Shakespeare are taken from *Love's Labours Lost* where they were composed by characters who were less than accomplished versifiers. The volume's remaining fifteen poems are by other poets (see Greenblatt, 235; Duncan-Jones, 1997, 2). Jaggard simply sought the material advantage to be had by putting Shakespeare's name on the title-page and thus attracting more readers and increasing profits. Nor was Jaggard's piracy and misattribution his sole transgression of this sort: he printed no fewer than three editions of *The Passionate Pilgrim*, the last of which appeared in 1612, that is, three years after Shakespeare's own volume of sonnets was published.

Just a year before the 1609 Quarto was published, there is, however, the evidence of Shakespeare's supervision of his sonnets manuscript. Shakespeare's fellow dramatist, Thomas Heywood, remarks in *An Apology for Actors* that Shakespeare has been "much offended" by William Jaggard "that altogether unknowne to him presumed to make so bold with his name" (sig. G4). That Jaggard repeated the original offense reflects both the financial incentive to do so as well as Shakespeare's inability to do anything about it except exercise some control over the 1609 edition in having the sonnets published "in his owne name." From such evidence, one of the sonnets' foremost editors, Katherine Duncan-Jones, concludes: "[T]here is every reason to believe that the 1609 Quarto publication of the Sonnets was authorized by Shakespeare himself" (1997, 34).

Although the volume contains a number of indisputable typographical errors, we have no proof that the shape, arrangement, and presentation of the sonnets in the 1609 Quarto were *not* printed according to Shakespeare's specifications. In fact, it is more likely to be the case that he did exercise some considerable authorial control over the printing of the poems, especially since he carefully supervised the printing of two earlier narrative poems, *Venus and Adonis* (1593) and *Lucrece* (1594). Further, specific sonnets, notably 12 and 60, which are respectively about the hours and the minutes on the clock, are numbered to reflect their subject matter. This is clearly a deliberate and not an accidental choice, and it is logical to assume that it was made by none other than the poet himself. In addition, the sonnets show an intense preoccupation with the immortality of verse, which similarly bespeaks a powerful investment in the manner in which the *Sonnets* appeared in print. Since at least some of the poems were already composed by 1589, the year of Francis Meres's remark about "honey-tongued Shakespeare," and his "sugared sonnets among his private friends," it must be that he had worked over them for nearly a decade.

CHAPTER 2

Identity

As we noted in the introduction, there are unusually intricate and intriguing problems about identity in Shakespeare's sonnets. These have excited curiosity, speculation, and conjecture throughout the centuries. Predominantly at issue is the obliquely identified Mr. W. H., the dedicatee designated by Thomas Thorpe, who appears to be one and the same person as the nameless young man whose identity is completely occluded in the sonnets themselves. Then there is the pressing matter of the poet in the sonnets, who may be a persona adopted for the fictional purposes of the poems and not a representation of Shakespeare himself. Additionally, there is the woman "colored ill," about whose identity we are indeed in the dark, and finally, there is the problem of identifying the rival poet or poets of Sonnets 78–80 and 82–6. To further complicate matters, although they are replete with pronouns and possessive adjectives – "I," "me," "mine," "myself," "you," "thee," "thou," "thine," "thy," "thyself" – the majority of the sonnets do not reveal the gender of the person to whom they are addressed.

The tensions around questions of identity in the sonnets arise from the fact that, on the one hand, they are written within the parameters of a distinct and well-established literary tradition, but, on the other hand, they do not have the kinds of direct literary sources that we find in relation both to other sonneteers of the era and, indeed, to most of Shakespeare's plays. Furthermore, as each generation of new readers is often surprised to discover, the poet in the sonnets describes not only his love for a man and a woman, but also the sexual involvement of these two with each other. This love triangle, extraordinary in the annals of the sonnet tradition, has fueled intense biographical speculation.

Whether the sonnets are wholly biographical or, conversely, wholly personal without being in the least biographical, this chapter will argue that the elusive identities presented in them are always first and foremost literary rather than biographical formations. That the poet, the youth, and the woman are all identities expressed and assumed with the shape and form of the sonnet makes it more important to establish the history of sonnet identity than to speculate about historical identity. However, there is an important distinction to be made here: to say that the identities of the figures in the sonnets are predominantly literary identities is not the same as saying that they are "made up" or "not real." Modern readers are much misled by our naïve yet quasi-scientific idea that things fall into one of two categories: fact (objective reality) or fiction ("made up" and thus untrue). "Fact" and "fiction" were not used in our modern sense in the period that Shakespeare was writing. *A Midsummer Night's Dream* refers to the essentially fictional and duplicitous nature of love poetry when Egeus tells the Duke that his daughter has been bewitched "with feigning voice verses of feigning love" (1.1.31). And while the "feigned" might be opposed to "truth," there was nothing like our straightforward notion that fiction not only is different from fact but also is opposed to it. Sir Philip Sidney's *Defense of Poesie* argued, for example, that this kind of invention, more than any purely technical expertise, was the very hallmark of the poet: "[I]t is not rhyming and versing that maketh a poet [. . .] But it is that feigning of notable images of virtues, vices, or what else, with that delightful teaching, which must be the right describing note to know a poet by." Despite Puritan rumblings about the dangers of lyricism and imagination, there was a pervasive belief that poetry might draw readers toward a higher order of truth, one that transcended the distinction between an objective reality and an imagined one.

That all the sexual and emotional dimensions of the sonnets have precedents and parallels in literary convention, even as their specific expression in Shakespeare's sonnets is quite unique, does not mean, then, that the texture of lived experience is merely a carefully wrought literary convention. Rather, it is to say that the verse form is embedded within a long history – the history of lyric poetry itself. The relationships in the sonnets can neither be wholly derived from nor reduced to mere convention, trope and topos. The vitality of lived emotion in the sonnets draws us inexorably toward its real-life antecedent, even when scant surviving documentary evidence limits our access there. What we must acknowledge is that all poetic conventions are ultimately derived from real-life models, and that poetry marks a discursive boundary between the subjective experience of love and desire and a shared human history of that experience. This liminal status is further exacerbated in the historical moment in which Shakespeare wrote because, as Colin Burrow has pointed out, the publication of the *Sonnets* in 1609 "powerfully reinforces this view of the sonnet as a form which was located at the intersection between private papers and printed record" (Burrow, 98). Because the history of poetry is in this complicated way coincident with the history of love, it is important to understand the history of lyrical identity before addressing the detective work aimed to establish the specific historical identities of Shakespeare's lovers that has occupied so many commentators on the sonnets.

Lyrical Identity

The formal shape of the sonnet convention in early modern England was defined in *Certain Notes of Instruction* (1587) by George Gascoigne: "I can best allow to call those sonnets which are fourteen lines, every line containing ten syllables. The first twelve do rhyme in staves of four lines by cross meter, and the last two rhyming together do conclude the whole" (288). This was the container for a range of tropes and themes that derived most significantly from the Italian *quattrocento* poet Francesco Petrarch (1304–74), who founded the dominant paradigm of the sonnet form in Italy. His great innovation was in using the sonnet as the vehicle for exquisite versification in the vernacular. Petrarch achieved extraordinary lyrical eloquence hitherto thought to belong only to Latin by using the Italian spoken by his contemporaries and became a model of stylistic elegance for all European vernacular languages. English was particularly unsuited to metrical and syntactic models of Latin and Greek poetry, and in the sixteenth century English poetry was revived only by the belated appropriation of Petrarch.[1] After visiting Italy in the service of Henry VIII in 1527, Sir Thomas Wyatt (1503–42) translated some of Petrarch's sonnets into English, and Henry Howard, Earl of Surrey (1517–47), used Petrarch as a model for English metrical formations. While these developments were monumentally significant in the course of English poetry, they were still within the confines of the elite literary culture of court circles, and nowhere approached the more motley urban audiences that Shakespeare was to reach with the sonnets in London in 1609. Even as late as the 1580s, Shakespeare's most important immediate precursor in the sonnet form was aristocratic. This was Sir Philip Sidney, a member of the powerful Pembroke family who penned *Astrophil and Stella* almost a decade before it was posthumously published in 1591.

While Shakespeare's sonnets are written within the conventions of the genre, they clearly deviate from the strictly elite, courtly, stylized literary precedents of Wyatt, Surrey, and Sidney. Shakespeare also differs from orthodox Petrarchanism in another signal respect, namely that conventionally, Petrarchan poetry involved the pursuit and idealization, first, of a woman, and, second, of a woman the poet could never attain. Petrarchan love was always unrequited and unconsummated, like Romeo's love for the "fair Rosaline" who has taken a vow of chastity in *Romeo and Juliet*. Petrarch's *Canzoniere* (literally, "songs"), also known as the *Rime Sparse* (literally, scattered rhyme), detail the poet's tormented love for Laura. Her trademark unavailability becomes crystalized when she dies, an event which does not end the sequence but simply shifts it to another register. Even before her death, the poet-lover is melancholy to the point of psychological disintegration, and the poems recount his inner anguish so as to make the interiority of the poet a new subject for literature, describing the changing moods and nuances of male desire.

In addressing these questions about poetic identity in the sonnets, it is important to bear in mind that the great achievement of the Petrarchan sonnet was its exploration of the interior, emotional world of the poet and that Wordsworth's oft quoted remark, "With this key Shakespeare unlocked his heart," might be true even if the rendition of those emotions involves imagined people or situations. Similarly, in a very real sense, Petrarch's *Canzoniere* were not "about" the elusive Laura, the ostensible "subject" of the poems, but were in every sense "about" Petrarch. That is, Petrarch and the poet's subjective identity – whether or not it correlated with the objective "facts" of his external, historical reality – were their real subject, and even the descriptions of Laura can be properly considered as projections of his own desires,

ideals, beliefs, and aspirations. Laura's very name is in Italian pronounced "L'aura," and is thus a pun on the Italian word for air, breath,
and breeze, and thus the vocality of poetic language:

> And blessed be all of the poetry
> I scattered, calling out my lady's name,
> And all the sighs, and tears, and the desire.
>
> (Canzone 61.9–11)

Petrarch's sonnets were originally sung to a lyre. Thus, the pun on
Laura's name draws the listener's attention to the lyrics as poetically
heightened acts of language, which in Petrarch's case represents not
only the shift from ordinary language to poetic language, but also the
movement from speech to song.

Petrarch's pursuit of the woman who has disdained him, his decision "to chase this lady who has turned in flight" (6.2), is also a poetic
aspiration symbolized by the emblem of laurel leaves (reflected still in
the title "poet laureate" for a nation's designated poet). Thus, "to reach
the laurel" (*"per venir al **lauro**"*) (6.12) is at once the attempt to attain
the fair Laura and a symbol of the poet's more purely literary objectives. In Canzone 23, Petrarch tells us that Laura and Cupid have
together changed him: "from living man they turned me to green
laurel" (*"d'uom vivo un **lauro** verde"*) (23.39). The poems written after
Laura's death are the ones in which she becomes most clearly an idea
in the poet's mind, an aspect of Petrarchan imagination:

> . . . I sang of you for many years
> now, as you see, I sing for you in tears –
> no, not in tears for you but for my loss.
>
> (282.9–11)

It is clearer in grief that the poetic expression is "all about Petrarch"
rather than really about Laura; but it remains the case that all along,
he has been writing about his own emotional upheaval for which
Laura is more the cipher than the true subject. For all that Petrarchanism marks the advent of a new (fundamentally masculine) interiority, or perhaps because of it, the reader is not permitted to see the
world from Laura's point of view. We come to know her only through
her external attributes, which unlike those of Shakespeare's "dark
lady" in Sonnet 130 are in no way idiosyncratic, individual, or unique:

she has eyes like diamonds, hair like gold, cheeks like roses, skin like alabaster, and teeth like pearls. Shakespeare's young man, in contrast, though described only as "fair," is very much fashioned within the poetic artifice of idealization that is the predominant characteristic of Petrarchanism. The series of rhetorical and lyrical conventions that comprised Petrarchanism was such that it was impossible to write (and perhaps even to love) outside them. Shakespeare's sonnets, while they do not simply conform to Petrarchan conventions, and indeed are often written against them, are always conceived *in relation* to them.

Questions of identity that the sonnets present us with, then, are crucially subject to the determinations of genre, and the elusive identities of Shakespeare's sonnets, far from being exempt from literary convention, are in fact produced by it. Shakespeare and his rivals and lovers probably correlate to real people in his experience of life in London before and after the turn of the sixteenth century, but it is the specifically *elusive* cast of identity that signals its insistently literary nature. In addressing the problem of identity in the sonnets, it is important to note that Shakespeare did not write the sonnets in a vacuum but within a genre with a strong literary tradition in which the identity of the addressee of the poem is inherently elusive. The fugitive and quasi-mystical identity sonnets invoke thus exceeds the rubrics of history and biography. In the lyrical tradition at least, the beloved has the capacity to figure forth a corporeal identity while simultaneously being possessed of a configuration of typically (though not always) ideal qualities beyond those that could reasonably be attached to any real historical person. Although we "know" the identity of Laura because the *Rime* names her as the poet's love, Petrarch's contemporaries questioned her existence. Similarly, Dante's passionate sonnet sequence *La vita nuova* (ca. 1292) was addressed to Beatrice Portinari, someone with whom he may have only had passing acquaintance while they were both children. While Shakespeare's Elizabethan contemporaries gave names to the women to whom their sonnets were addressed, such as Elizabeth (Edmund Spenser's future wife Elizabeth Boyle who is addressed in the *Amoretti*) and Stella (Sidney's Lady Penelope Rich), it is not clear that these names, even when they appear to allude to real, historical figures, reflected actual people in actual relationships, but were, rather, imaginative fantasies.

Shakespeare's young man, who illustrates the notorious problem of establishing identity as well as the tantalizing biographical and autobiographical intimations of poetry, must be considered within this tradition. We are confronted, on the one hand, by the supremely lifelike rendition of specific individual identity in all its insistent particularity, and, on the other, by anonymity or disputed identity. As we have noted, the difficulty in ascertaining true identity is not merely the product of problematic or missing historical data but is crucially produced by the ways in which the poet has used the conventions and techniques of his medium in order to articulate an ideal, even while taking an ostensibly objective and individualized perspective on his subject. As a genre, sonnets constitute the fruits of an encounter between the poet, or the poet's persona, and the object of his address on the one hand, and, on the other, the elusive identity of *the beloved*, the *inamorata* who conforms to the specifications of type precisely because she is *like no other*. The disjunction between "actual identity," even where such an identity is explicitly assigned, and the lyrical construction of the beloved reveals the poet's (and not necessarily the author's) fantasy about the object of his adoration. Not infrequently, the beloved, like the woman who has been identified as Petrarch's Laura, an apparently homely matron of Avignon who gave birth to no fewer than ten children (none of them Petrarch's), or Sir Philip Sidney's "Stella," Lady Penelope Rich, who divorced her husband and bore two illegitimate children (neither of them Sidney's since she was never sexually involved with him), is an iconic and rather distant cousin of the real woman she purports to represent.

In terms of this lyrical rather than straightforwardly historical order of reality, even before the sonnet form arrived in Italy to appear in the great vernacular works of Dante and Petrarch, there was, then, a puzzling connection between biographical specificity and aesthetic ideal. The sonnet tradition originates in the twelfth-century Provençal tradition of the heretical troubadours of Languedoc. *Dompna*, the langue d'oc for *Domina* (the feminine counterpart of *Dominus*, Lord), participates in the iconography of the Virgin Mary, the cult of Mary Magdalen, and the pagan mother goddess. In other words, we are looking not just for a real person but also for the human reality behind the lyrical hyperbole, the elevated language, and the exalted philosophical – and even divine – ideal. While Shakespeare's sonnets are securely secular poems, the youth's quasi-divine characteristics appear nonetheless, notably, for example, in his "blessed shape" in Sonnet 53, and in his status as "better angel" in Sonnet 144.

It is not, of course, only the historical identity of the young man that is at stake in the sonnets but also the sexual identity of Shakespeare himself. There is a long critical and editorial tradition of homophobia in relation to the sonnets because, especially in previous generations, readers could not bring themselves to believe that the greatest poet in the English language might have had sexual relations with another man. Infamously, one editor, John Benson (d. 1667), a bookseller, produced a volume of the sonnets entitled *Poems* in 1640, in which he not only rearranged the sonnets and excised several of them altogether, but also invented titles such as "The glory of beauty" and "The benefit of friendship." He also changed "boy" in Sonnet 108 to "love," apparently in order to preserve Shakespeare from what he may have deemed to be the "taint" of sodomy (de Grazia, 89–90). Thus, "friend" in 104 is changed to "love." The eighteenth-century editor George Steevens, who reprinted the sonnets in 1766 with a collection of early quartos, condemned Sonnet 20 in particular with what he read as the poet's frank admission of sexual interest in the young man as "the master mistress of my passion," saying, "It is impossible to read without an equal mixture of disgust and indignation" (Rollins, I, 55). Similarly, Hermann Conrad claimed it was a moral duty to show that the sonnets had nothing to do with the "loathsome, sensual degeneracy of love among friends that antiquity unfortunately knew" (quoted Rollins, II, 233).

Even within the story of the sonnets, the issue of sexual identity is complicated by the fact that the first seventeen sonnets urge the young man to reproduce, an injunction incompatible with the desire for sexual exclusivity one might expect from an infatuated lover. In contrast to these poems, Sonnets 127–52, addressed to the unknown woman, bespeak the somewhat misogynist loathing of the wounded lover rather than the admiration and praise represented by the sonnets that appear earlier in the volume. Interestingly, the poet's disgust about sex with a woman has not historically aroused the indignation or condemnation that has been provoked by the sonnets' intimations of same-sex desire. Be that as it may, questions of identity are further compounded by the fact that Sonnets 40–2, 133, 134, and 144 reveal that the poet is involved in an acutely painful love triangle. In response to these controversies, and in particular to the debate about Shakespeare's putative homosexuality, Stephen Booth effectively scotched biographical speculation with the now famous remark that: "William Shakespeare was almost certainly homosexual, bisexual, or heterosexual. The sonnets provide no evidence on the matter" (Booth, 1977, 548). That statement is unequivocally correct; however, it is also the case that *the poet* of the sonnets desires a young man in ways that allude to a decided and specifically sexual desire, and is enamored of a woman who both fascinates and repels him.

Shakespeare is not alone among Renaissance poets in writing about the love between men. Famously, although Shakespeare probably had no knowledge of it, the Italian artist and poet Michelangelo, a professed celibate, wrote sonnets about his erotic longings for a number of young men, most notably Tommaso Cavalieri. He also wrote passionately about his platonic love for Vittoria Colonna, as well as sonnets to another enigmatic and unidentified addressee, who seems to be a purely fictional figure, the beautiful cruel lady, *la donna bella y cruella*. Michelangelo's sonnets were published in an expurgated and editorially butchered form by his grandnephew in 1623. Indeed, in relation to other important literary traditions, such as pastoral, there is also a convention of expressing the love between men, and these are the conventions Shakespeare would have known well. Further, in the history of poetry, and particularly in the massively influential Roman elegy, homosexual relationships and married mistresses were not particularly unusual. Even the vigorously heterosexual Ovid (Shakespeare's favorite poet) glances casually at a reference to homoerotic experience: "I hate it unless both lovers reach a climax: / That's why I don't much go for boys" (*Ars Amatoria* 2.683–4, trans. Green). Homoerotic love was an aspect of pastoral convention and was explored in Elizabethan England in Edmund Spenser's *Shepherd's Calendar*, published in 1579. Spenser's sonnet sequence, the *Amoretti* (1595), on the other hand, details his courtship of Elizabeth Boyle, the woman he married in 1594. Far from representing the (heterosexual) norm, however, Spenser's sonnets are also decidedly unusual, but for entirely different reasons from those of Shakespeare's, namely that the end of Spenser's pursuit was marriage. The objective of legitimate conjugal felicity was a marked contrast from the lyrical catalog of torment, frustration, and rejection that had characterized the genre since Petrarch. Thus, what was novel about Spenser's sonnets was that they were about the road to emotional and erotic fulfillment within Christian marriage in its ideal form.

In contrast to Spenser's *Amoretti*, one thing we can be certain of at least in relation to Shakespeare is that the sonnets are not about Shakespeare's wife. (Even here, however, there is a literary precedent in that Dante did not address the *Vita nuova* to his wife, Gemma Donati.) Shakespeare married Anne Hathaway in 1582 though he did not long remain with her in Stratford after their marriage; nor was he at home when his only son, Hamnet, died in 1596 aged 11, and he notoriously bequeathed Anne his second best bed. Whatever Shakespeare's sexuality, he was an absent husband and father much of the time. Since he returned to Stratford-upon-Avon a wealthy man, able to purchase the grand property of New Place, we can only speculate as to whether his long absences in London were the result of preference or necessity, but certainly the capital would have allowed him greater sexual as well as artistic license than would have been possible in the confines of his native place.

There is one exception, however, to the extramarital tenor of Shakespeare's sonnets. In Sonnet 145, the penultimate line suggests a pun on his wife's name, Anne Hathaway, pronounced "Hattaway": " 'I hate' from 'hate' away she threw" (Gurr, 221–6). Written in octosyllabic lines, that is, with eight rather than the usual ten syllables of iambic pentameter to a line, this poem is probably a very early and metrically experimental example of Shakespeare's verse. It may even date from the period in 1582 when Shakespeare, only 18 years old, was wooing his future wife, aged 26, whom he married after she became pregnant. Powerful social and legal forces in early modern England conspired to compel matrimony in such cases – cases of bastardy, in particular, routinely went to court. It is possible that Shakespeare and Anne's nuptials may have been the result of a similar coercion of people and circumstances more than a genuine expression of the poet's own choice. Once again, we know only the fact that there was little financial incentive to marry Anne, who had a rather paltry dowry of ten marks. We know, therefore, that Shakespeare did not marry for money, but unfortunately, we cannot prove that he married for love. All we have to go on is this poem:

> Those lips that Loves own hand did make,
> Breath'd forth the sound that said I hate,

To me that languished for her sake:
But when she saw my woefull state,
Straight in her heart did mercy come,
Chiding that tongue that ever sweet,
Was used in giving gentle doom:
And taught it thus a new to greet:
I hate she altered with an end,
That follow'd it as gentle day,
Doth follow night who like a fiend
From heaven to hell is flown away.
   I hate, from **hate away** she threw,
   And sav'd my life saying not you.
                (Sonnet 145, my emphasis)

Significantly, with the single exception of John Kerrigan who calls this "a pretty trifle which has been much abused" (376), critics have otherwise agreed that it is the least interesting and accomplished of all of Shakespeare's sonnets. The line of reasoning here implies that Anne, alas, does not seem to have had it in her power to attract her husband's best, either early on in matters of poetry, or subsequently in matters of furniture. For all the critical condemnation it has attracted, this is a witty and clever poem. The pat rhymes may betray a lesser degree of technical accomplishment so evident in the other sonnets. However, here, the rhymes, while essentially (and obviously) relationships of sound, suggest a range of logical and semantic relationships as echoes of the human relationship to which they refer. The rhymes of Sonnet 145 show us how relationships are wrought in language. For the first three lines, the exchange between the poet and the mistress follows the Petrarchan pattern all too predictably, even though the charming, dramatic representation of a lover's tiff is a rather tamer version of the emotional cataclysms that Laura's indifference induces in Petrarch. Rather, it resembles more closely the benign ructions of Spenser's quarrels with Elizabeth Boyle, who finds the poet annoying and locks him out in the rain. Here in Sonnet 145, the lady has uttered, with lips made by Cupid ("Love") himself, something that threatens to destroy the poet's emotional equilibrium – she has said that she hates rather than that she loves him. The hyperbolic language, such as the insertion of the mythic origin of the woman's mouth, and the poet's reaction – melancholy, languishing – make for an amusing vignette. But unlike the Petrarchan lady, who is the paradigmatic *belle dame sans*

merci, this lady shows mercy, by qualifying her utterance: "Not you."
A tiny, insignificant exchange is amplified with a history of origins in
line 1, and then an elaborate account which extrapolates the woman's
reaction to have her consult with various organs of her anatomy: her
heart, her tongue. Finally, her mercy is figured as a kind of ambassa-
dor who has done the rounds of diplomacy in order to produce the
benign final couplet. The anxious lover's deep reprieve allowed by the
"not you" is figured in grandiose terms as the distinction between hell
and heaven, day and night.

While most commentators dismiss this poem as a lightweight juve-
nile effort on Shakespeare's part, Sonnet 145 remains one of the
strongest pieces of evidence we have for a biographical reading of the
sonnets. Further, this evidence is embedded within the sonnet itself
and does not require resort to extraneous "evidence" (of which there
is nothing but dearth), or more accurately, critical conjecture. The allusion to "Hathaway" is notable in part because it identifies the poet with
Shakespeare himself. We cannot assume, of course, that because this
is the case in one poem it is also the case in all the rest. We are still
compelled to ask whether the "I" of the sonnets represents the real
historical person, William Shakespeare, or a poetic "persona," that is,
a fictive identity assumed for wholly lyrical or imaginary purposes.
Since the one thing we know about the sonnets is that they are first
and foremost literary productions rather than factual or historical ones,
it is very likely that the "I" of the sonnets is a reflection of both the
real and imagined identity of the poet.

However, as we have noted, unlike Petrarch and the English Petrar-
chists, Shakespeare does not give the people of his poems names.
Indeed, the only name in the sonnets, even if it refers, as some critics,
perhaps straining common sense, have argued, to someone else
(allegedly to one of the woman's other lovers, also called Will), is also
coincident with the poet's own, rendered in the final couplet of Sonnet
136 as:

> Make but my name thy love, and love that still,
> And then thou lovest me for my name is *Will*.
> (136.12–14)

In the course of two sonnets, 135 and 136, the name "Will" and puns
upon it alluding variously to sexual desire, to the penis ("Will" was

the early modern equivalent of giving the male organ a proper name, such as "Johnson" or "John Thomas"), or to the vagina, occur no fewer than twenty times, and it is not only capitalized like a proper name but also italicized ten times:

> Whoever hath her wish, thou hast thy *Will*,
> And *Will* to boot, and *Will* in over-plus;
> More than enough am I that vexed thee still,
> To thy sweet will making addition thus.
> Wilt thou, whose will is large and spacious,
> Not once vouchsafe to hide my will in thine?
> Shall will in others seem right gracious,
> And in my will no fair acceptance shine?
> The sea, all water, yet receives rain still,
> And in abundance addeth to his store;
> So thou, being rich in *Will*, add to thy *Will*
> One will of mine, to make thy large *Will* more.
> Let no unkind, no fair beseechers kill;
> Think all but one, and me in that one *Will*.
> (Sonnet 135)

The shift from "wish" to "Will" in the first line of the poem suggests the move from desire to physical consummation. "Over-plus" means the woman has had sexual possession of the speaker to the point of surfeit and even that the dimensions of his tumescent member have overwhelmed her. It is not too far off the mark to suggest that this poem is all about size: "More than enough am I that vex thee still." This line jokingly refers to sexual chafing: the vexing or rubbing that stimulates sexual excitement. That is, other women may get what they want, but the poet's lover gets him, in all the specificity and particularity of his identity and his sexual presence in her body. The woman has emotional and sexual possession of her lover, and she can be sure of his capacity to sustain an erection. While this poem is a verbal game on this range of bawdy associations, it also reveals the poet's anxiety about the woman's acceptance of him. Certainly, she has received him sexually, "more than enough," and he intimates that other women have accepted him sexually: "Shall will [penis] in others seem right gracious . . . ?" Conversely, it could mean that sexual intercourse in general receives women's approval and that their lovers sexually satisfy other unspecified women. The poet deals with his insecurities by noting that the woman's sexual capaciousness, expressed in a bawdy phrase that refers explicitly to the dimensions of her sexual orifice ("thy will is large"), can surely accommodate him too. The final couplet urges her to accept all the men who want to copulate with her because all expressions of desire (Will) are really figurations of his desire and of him. It is cunning, perhaps deliberately self-deluding logic, a kind of mathematical rationalization of the fact that the poet has not secured exclusive sexual access to the woman he desires.

This poem is, of course, about "willfulness," about being bound and determined to achieve a specific, and in this case, sexual objective. The tenor of this poem is, like a number of other sonnets in the 1609 Quarto, decidedly un-Petrarchan. Here the poet does not take up the Petrarchan posture of languishing as he does in 145 – a much more conventional poem from the perspective of the sonnet tradition as a whole. His sexual determination rather resembles the Roman poet Ovid, whose frank representation of sexual desire both shocked and fascinated Renaissance readers. When Francis Meres remarked on the manuscript circulation of Shakespeare's "sugared sonnets among his private friends," he also made a telling critical remark, one that gets overshadowed by the alleged "mystery" of when and to whom they were written. Meres's perceptive observation is that "As the soul of Euphorbus was thought to live in Pythagoras: so the sweet witty soul of *Ovid* lives in mellifluous & honey-tongued Shakespeare, witness his *Venus and Adonis*, his *Lucrece*, his sugared Sonnets among his private friends, &c." There is no mystery about Shakespeare's love of Ovid whose mellifluous, amorous Latin verse was known to every Elizabethan schoolboy: he quotes the ancient poet more than any other. Ovid, of course, was writing long before the development of the sonnet, but for all that, his love elegies raised issues about whether great poetic achievements associated with momentous public issues and grand epic themes could be effected on the smaller scale of the private world and in smaller poetic dimensions. Size matters in the poetic sense as well as the sexual one: Ovid wrote in the feminized and "minuscule" (*Amores* 3.1.41) elegiac meter, which takes as its subject loving women rather than epic meter and fighting men. Ovid tells us at the opening of the *Amores* that he intended to write an epic, but that Cupid wounded him, so "Goodbye to martial epic, and epic meter too!" (1.1.28). Indeed, the beginning of each of the three books of the *Amores* offers an account of Ovid's repeated and invariably failed attempts to write high-flown verse about gods, heroes, and war, only to end up writing about the sublime but terrestrial issues of sex, women, and love. Thus, the "Will" of the sonnets as a poetic identity is immensely indebted to Shakespeare's ancient precursor.

In the *Amores*, Ovid writes:

> If one girl can drain my powers
>   Fair enough – but if she can't, I'll take two.
> I can stand the strain. My limbs may be thin, but they're wiry;
>   Though I'm a lightweight, I'm hard –
> And virility feeds on sex, is boosted by practice;
>   No girl's ever complained about *my* technique.
> Often enough I have spent the whole night in pleasure, yet still been
>   Fit as a fighting cock next day.
>
> (*Amores* 2.21–8, trans. Green)

Ovid is a model of the sexually explicit, but more than that, his exuberant, sexually indefatigable persona, while it undoubtedly comports with some of the features of the poet's actual life, is also the model of a poetry which, for all that it details what purports to be direct personal experience, finds its origins in literature as much as in life.

One way or another, in fact, Shakespeare thought a great deal about wills: three of his only six surviving signatures appear on the only genuinely biographical document that records desires we can unequivocally ascribe to him. These are on his actual will – that is, the same document in which he parcels out his property and bequeaths his second best bed to his wife. It is so tempting to extrapolate the details of Shakespeare's emotional life from a document that is essentially an itinerary of his possessions that we tend to overlook the fact that it is, overall, typical and unremarkable when compared to others of this era. Shakespeare was principally concerned in his will to keep his property (lands and buildings) intact down the generations, and for this reason decreed that it should go to his daughter Susanna's eldest son: "the first son of her body lawfully issuing and to the heirs males of the body of the said first son lawfully issuing" (Schoenbaum, 21). A will in this sense of course conveys the desires of the dead to the living, and imposes its terms upon them in ways that are legally binding. The other sense of "will" was one Shakespeare had played upon in the title of one of his most loved comedies, *Twelfth Night: Or What you Will* (ca. 1601–2). This is a play also about erotic desire and sexual fantasy ("what you will" translates into modern parlance as "whatever you want"), and about the rather flexible connection between its hetero and homoerotic manifestations. The central character is Viola, who is, implausibly, an "identical" yet fraternal twin to her brother Sebastian. These siblings are, it seems, undistinguishable except by genital anatomy, so that when Viola dons male apparel there is simply no telling them apart: "One face, one voice, one habit, and two persons!" (5.1.208). The insistence that gender, which we usually take to be the definitive marker of identity, might actually provide very little real distinction between two people is the source of the comedy in this play. Indeed, there is a sense in which the twins, Viola and Sebastian, present, almost like a reversible raincoat, a single but doubled-sided identity. Further, this reversibility implies a sexual playfulness of the type that we see in Sonnet 135, where there is a ludic interchangeability between the female and male components of "will."

While the connection between "will" in the sense of "last will and testament" and "will" in the sense of desire and wish fulfillment may seem simply a matter of semantic coincidence to us, early moderns made the connection quite explicit. A well-known proverb cited by Morris Tilley in his famous book of aphorisms made a pun on both these meanings of "will" (726). This pair of "will" sonnets, then, is heavily freighted with poetic identity, even if that identity is entangled in complex ways with questions about the transmission of property, as well as the physical anatomy of desire, both the poet's own and that of the woman's and her other sexual partners.

Who's That Lady?

We have already discerned the identity of one lady in the sonnets, that is to say, Anne Hathaway of Sonnet 145. We should derive as much satisfaction from this as we are able because this is the closest to a definitive identification we can come in the sonnets. Because we have only the poems to go on, it is as well to start there. Sonnet 145 comes directly after one of the darkest poems in the volume, a poem that was first published in the pirated volume, *The Passionate Pilgrim*, of 1599:

> Two loves I have of comfort and despair,
> Which like two spirits do suggest me still:
> The better angel is a man right fair,
> The worser spirit a woman colored ill.
> To win me soon to hell, my female evil,
> Tempteth my better angel from my side,
> And would corrupt my saint to be a devil,
> Wooing his purity with her foul pride.
> And whether that my angel be turned fiend,
> Suspect I may, yet not directly tell;
> But being both from me, both to each friend,
> I guess one angel in another's hell:
>   Yet this shall I ne'er know, but live in doubt,
>   Till my bad angel fire my good one out.
>
>   (Sonnet 144)

This sonnet, the famous love triangle lyric, addresses the suspected infidelity of the poet's female lover with the man he loves. That Sonnet 145 follows immediately after it registers an abrupt change in tone, and if we read the poems in order, the poet, like the reader, finds consolation and relief in 145, a poem where the fiend is banished, "From heaven to hell is flown away," after the torment of 144. These poems most likely refer to two different women, but even their sequence conspires to construct a composite sonnet identity, to lead us away from historical identification and specificity even as we press our noses up against the window of emotional particularity. The point here is not chronological sequence but rather the subjective regimes of emotional logic, memory, and psychological impression. The irresistible conclusion is, as John Berryman put it in *The Freedom of the Poet*, "When Shakespeare wrote, 'Two loves I have,' reader, he was *not kidding*" (quoted Vendler, 605).

Sonnet 144 is an astonishing poem on every front. Its revelations are shocking, not even primarily from the moral point of view, but from the Petrarchan one. Shakespeare's "woman colored ill" is far from being sexually unattainable as predicated by the tradition of aristocratic love poetry. Indeed, the most important aspect of the woman's identity from both a poetic and a social perspective is that she is decidedly *not* aristocratic, and indeed, Shakespeare does not even try to make the sonnets conform to the prescriptions of an aristocratic sequence. However, the identities expressed in this poem are also dramatic and archetypal. The angel and the devil refer to the psychomachia of medieval mystery plays, and there is a sense in which we are in the quasi-metaphysical realm of the broadest of categories – good and evil, male and female. In this sense, Sonnet 144 spans the antipodes of erotic experience which are, at one extreme, self-determining, "willful," conscious matters of social identity, and, at the other, they are the unconscious, instinctive forces that can seem in conflict with or even extraneous to social identity. However, the emotional force of the poem grounds these grand abstractions in the particularity of betrayal, and lest we take flight in the airy reaches of archetype, it is worth considering one of the most trenchant critical comments made on the sonnets about the woman colored ill, and it is perhaps also notable that it was made by a female editor, Katherine Duncan-Jones: "The so-called dark-lady sonnets constitute a poetic equivalent of the beating up of whores that was such a popular holiday pastime for young men of high status" (Duncan-Jones, 2001, 215). Certainly, the poet avers that he has contracted venereal disease from the woman he has idolized:

> For I have sworn thee fair, and thought thee bright,
> Who art as black as hell, as dark as night.
>
> (Sonnet 147.13–14)

The woman's aspect is infernal – she is repeatedly associated with both hell and the nether regions of the body, and her darkness is moral as much as physical. These issues merit the further consideration we will give them later, but for now, it is important to grasp what significance the images of venereal disease, blackness, and hell have for the specific question of identity.

We know in other words *what* the woman *is like*, or rather what the poet says she is like, but we do not know *who she is*. Sonnet 152 tells us that she has broken her "bed vows," presumably a reference that she has broken her wedding vows by committing adultery with the poet. We also learn that she is musical in Sonnet 128, "when thou, my music, music play'st" (128.1), where she plays the virginals (a highly sexualized activity), a precursor of the modern instrument, the piano. However, we do not really know what she looks like, and whether she is of African descent or simply dark-haired, although "black" was then commonly used to refer to dark hair and dark complexions rather than to a specifically racial designation as it is today.

Because of the numerous references to venereal disease and darkness, one candidate is Luce Morgan, known as Lucy Negro, who worked out of a brothel in Clerkenwell. Another is Mary Fitton, an aristocratic lady who was one of Queen Elizabeth's maids of honor, though a surviving portrait shows her to be a very fair-skinned brunette, and definitely a "lady" rather than the "woman" Shakespeare describes. She had a child by the Earl of Pembroke, William Herbert (1580–1630), who because his initials are W. H. has been proposed (implausibly, in view of his title) as the dedicatee of the sonnets. A more intriguing possibility, for which there is once again, alas, no evidence, is Amelia Lanyer, a member of an Italian family of court musicians who was the mistress of Lord Hunsdon, patron of the Lord Chamberlain's Men, Shakespeare's acting company. When she got pregnant by Hunsdon, she was promptly married off elsewhere. Crucially, however, Lanyer was a poet of some considerable talent and potentially someone of dark, Mediterranean complexion. Her birth family's coat of arms was the mulberry tree, in Latin, *morus*, and a pun on "Moor" (Wood, 201).

My Lovely Boy

Oscar Wilde states the problem of the young man's identity most succinctly: "The problem . . . was this: Who was that young man of Shakespeare's day who, without being of noble birth or even of noble nature, was addressed by him in terms of such passionate adoration that we can but wonder at the strange worship, and are almost afraid to turn the key that unlocks the mystery of the poet's heart. Who was he whose physical beauty was such that it became the corner-stone of Shakespeare's art, the very source of Shakespeare's inspiration, the very incarnation of Shakespeare's dreams?" (Wilde, 30).

Ironically in Sonnet 81, the poet claims that "Your name from hence immortal life shall have / Though I (once gone) to all the world must die" (81.4–5). We should not, however, assume that Shakespeare meant this ironically. Clearly, if the young man had some social standing (albeit not a title, as we must infer from the "Mr." in Mr. W. H.), he would have every expectation of being remembered, while Shakespeare himself, though he hoped his verse would live on, might never have anticipated that his life would be of more interest than that of his addressee.

There are strong indications in the sonnets that the fair young man is of a considerably higher social status than the poet. Candidates for this role have included Henry Wriothesley, Earl of Southampton (1573–1624), who, like the young man, resisted marriage. When William Cecil, Lord Burghley, the queen's chief minister and the most powerful man in England, found that his own ward, Wriothesley, refused to marry Lady Elizabeth Vere, Burghley's own granddaughter, in 1591, he fined him the then enormous sum of £5,000. In that same year, John Clapham, at the instigation of his master, Lord Burghley, dedicated a Latin poem, *Narcissus*, which was the mythic story that tells of the dangers of self-love. The opening sonnets of the 1609 Quarto indeed develop a similar theme and explicitly refer to Narcissus. The references to "Rose" in the first sonnet were thought to be connected with the name "Wriothesley," because the first letter is silent and because certain of his descendants claimed it was pronounced "Rosely." Historians who argue that the name was in fact pronounced, less glamorously, "Risley" have rebutted this claim.[2]

Even if Southampton was the young man, given that Shakespeare was not in Burghley's service it seems odd that he would have urged his patron to marry in Sonnets 1–17 in the face of Southampton's implacable opposition to matrimony at this time. (Southampton finally did marry the already pregnant Elizabeth Vernon in 1597/8 when he was 25.) Further, if Shakespeare had intended to persuade Southampton to marry Lady Elizabeth Vere in particular and not just to accept the general proposition of marriage, one would expect a more defined sense of his proposed bride instead of the extremely vague and shadowy intimation of the "womb" bearer we are given. Southampton had indeed protested to Burghley that he objected to the idea of marriage in general rather than to Lady Vere in particular. This is likely to have been diplomacy on Southampton's part: it would surely have been unwise to tell the most powerful man in England that one found the prospect of marrying his granddaughter, Cecil's own flesh and blood, repugnant, whether for personal reasons or perhaps even for reasons of religious incompatibility. Even if Southampton's excuse had been true, such generalized objections made in the abstract are usually overcome when a specific, concrete object of affection presents itself. Southampton had begged his guardian reprieve from marriage for one year on grounds of his youth: "this generall answere that your Lordship was this last winter pleased to yield unto him a further respite

of one year to answer resolutely in respect of his young years"
(Akrigg, 32).

A further problem with the identification of Southampton as the
young man of Shakespeare's sonnets is that his initials are H. W., not
W. H., and that, even if we assume that the initials were inverted in a
printer's error, Southampton, like Herbert, the third Earl of Pembroke,
would not have been referred to, especially in a society as obsessed
with social status as was the early seventeenth century, as "Mr." Pembroke's life fits the profile of the sonnets: reluctant to marry as a young
man, he then had an affair with Mary Fitton, whom he got pregnant
in 1601. Fitton was one of a succession of well-born young women
whom Herbert had refused to marry. In 1595, marriage negotiations
between young Herbert, who did not become Earl of Pembroke until
his father's death in January 1601, and Elizabeth, the daughter of Sir
George Carey, collapsed because of his "not liking her." He was,
however, only 15 years old in 1595 and perhaps wisely reluctant to
be so precipitously pressed into matrimony. Again, in 1597, when
Herbert was only 17, a match was foiled between him and another of
Lord Burghley's granddaughters, Bridget Vere, and in 1599 Herbert
turned down the prospect of marriage with the Earl of Nottingham's
niece. J. Dover Wilson among others has claimed that there are seventeen sonnets devoted to the theme of persuading the young man to
marry because Shakespeare had been hired to urge Herbert to marry
as he reached his seventeenth birthday in April (Wilson, xcix–ci).
However, reluctance to marry was not in itself extraordinary. Marriage
negotiations were frequently protracted affairs, in part because when
the nobility were of the party, these were essentially dynastic mergers
in which the stakes for power, wealth, and property were signally high.
What makes Herbert's case unusual is that he was imprisoned at the
Fleet (a gaol south of the Thames) for his sexual misdemeanors with
Fitton and thereafter banished from court.

While casting around for candidates may not have brought scholars to a definitive identification of the people who inspired the sonnets,
provided it does not lead readers into the truly outrageous realms of
ahistorical speculation such conjecture can take us further into the
world in which they were written. Herein, I believe, lies its principal
– and arguably sole – value. A more manageable, even more pedes-
trian question about the sonnets might bring us nearer the mark. This
question approaches the matter from a different angle altogether, not

who Shakespeare was in love with, but rather what was he reading, and more to the point, where was he reading it? This would bring us back into the circle of the Earl of Southampton whom Shakespeare probably met in around 1592, when, having graduated from Cambridge University, Southampton was studying law at Gray's Inn. The Inns of Court offered a high concentration of educated young men who were interested in literature and the arts. Not only were students at the Inns of Court avid theatregoers, but plays were also performed in their own halls. For example, Shakespeare's *The Comedy of Errors* was performed at Gray's Inn during the Christmas festivities of 1594 (Whitworth, 7–9). Further, the students themselves put on performances during periods of festivity. Shakespeare then had a number of connections with Gray's Inn in particular, and a compelling reason he might have had to go there would have been its library. The libraries of the Inns of Court contained far more than legal books and documents, and Shakespeare, especially in his early years in London as a playwright, must have had recourse to a library. Much of the library of Gray's Inn does not survive today, but in the 1960s the Canadian scholar Leslie Hotson claimed to have proven that the young man was William Hatcliffe, who had played the role of the Lord of Purpoole in an entertainment at Gray's Inn. His case is fanciful and overstated in many regards, but it is one whose merits have at least as much to recommend them as the Southampton and Pembroke theses.

Conclusion

As readers of the sonnets, we simply have to learn to live with a considerable degree of ambiguity and uncertainty. We are on no surer ground in identifying the rival poets, where there is no evidence at all, despite a wealth of speculation.[3] The problems of identity with which the sonnets confront us cannot be "solved" or "resolved" over time, no matter what new information surfaces, because the enigma of identity they contain is not solely a matter of missing historical information. Certain of the ambiguities of identity bespeak the very nature of the sonnet form, not to mention the opacity of the beloved in relation to the beloved that necessarily obtains in any human relationship.

CHAPTER 3

Beauty

Whether the sonnets disclose anything about Shakespeare's own sexual predilections is a matter for critical debate. What is beyond doubt, however, as this chapter will argue, is that the poems reveal that the principal object of their meditation on beauty is the idealized young man and not the woman colored ill. Beauty in the sonnets is unequivocally a masculine attribute and a signal of class status. As Margreta de Grazia puts it: "Fair is the distinguishing attribute of the dominant class" (de Grazia, 101). However, ideal beauty in the sonnets is male beauty with a twist: the beautiful young man looks like a woman. Since the young man sonnets conform in part to the poetry of praise required of a system of patronage where the poet wrote for the pleasure of an individual who was willing to pay for it, this might seem a rather surprising tack for Shakespeare to take with his young patron. However, the beauty of the androgyne or the hermaphrodite was also an aesthetic ideal to which literary representations of beauty might aspire. Such fused gender identities were understood, from an aesthetic point of view, to be manifestations of beauty that transcended gender distinction by incorporating the best features of both sexes.

In the latter part of the Quarto, the unconventional attractions and the inexplicable sexual magnetism of the woman represent the exploration of a kind of anti-aesthetic that reinvigorates the well-worn codes of Petrarchan lyrical hyperbole by first unsettling them.

Breeding Beauty

"From fairest creatures we desire increase, / That thereby beauty's *Rose* might never die" begins the first poem of the 1609 Quarto, a statement which can be understood as the first articulation of the sonnets' aesthetic agenda, namely to expand, amplify, and perpetuate the presence and condition of beauty in the world. These remarkable first lines also represent the idea that death is the mainspring of human creativity, fueling the drive toward survival and reproduction. Yet, these lines do not bespeak the mundane ambition to secure the continuity of human existence. Proposing first the natural appreciation of beauty: "From fairest creatures we desire increase," the aspiration expressed here is to sustain and perpetuate, not just life in any form, but life in its most aesthetically intensified manifestation. This enhanced beauty may even be ornamented, since the rose is not only the flowering or fullest expression of beauty but also its accentuation and adornment: "beauty's *Rose*." From this perspective, however, "beauty's *Rose*" intimates something beyond the sphere of purely natural reproduction, suggesting the realms of artifice, and thus specifically artistic manifestations of beauty. This is what the Earl of Arundel's librarian Franciscus Junius refers to in *De Pictura Veterum* (1637), or in its English version of 1638, *The Painting of the Ancients*, as "the *inbred* delight men take in the imitation of the works of Nature" (my emphasis). The general proposition of that first line, the natural appetite for more beauty, for "breeding" beauty, is one of the key themes of the sonnets: the absolute artistic and biological necessity of reproduction. For the problem with beauty, here and throughout the Quarto, is that beauty simply cannot sustain itself. Its inherent fragility is that it is subject to change, time, and death. This is not a problem in relation to material objects: they survive lifetimes and are handed down from generation to generation, long outlasting their original owners. So while material objects may suffer decay or loss, their capacity for duration far exceeds that of human beings, whose demise is not merely possible, but inevitable. In this, we light upon the central characteristic of the sonnets' aesthetic. That is, beauty, by definition, is living, not dead. Inert matter, no matter how carefully wrought, is just lifeless and defunct dross. The only thing that has right to the title of beauty is that which is breathing, pulsating, and alive. Beauty manifests this spark of life itself. One of the foundational arguments of the sonnets is that great art is *living* art, as the poet has it in Sonnet 81: "When all the breathers of this world are dead / You still shall live" (81.11–12). Here, in the pun on "breathers" and "breeders," art outstrips biology in the longevity stakes.

At this point in the Quarto, that is, a mere two lines into the first sonnet, Shakespeare has already conveyed a staggering amount of information to the reader. The rather generalized proposition about the innate human desire for beauty covers issues pertaining both to life in general and to art in particular. *"Rose,"* especially capitalized and italicized as it is in the 1609 Quarto, as we noted above is arguably a pun on the name "Wriothesley," the family name of the Earl of Southampton, who was Shakespeare's patron when he wrote the narrative poems *Venus and Adonis* (1593) and *Lucrece* (1594). *"Rose,"* by virtue of its typesetting, fairly leaps off the page. It may do so either by the author's deliberate intent or by an otherwise unmotivated compositor's decision in the print shop. However, since this is the earliest surviving version of Shakespeare's first sonnet, we cannot in good conscience ignore its visual prominence – even though most modern editors have done precisely that. Even if the capitalized, italicized rose is the result of the whim of a compositor, it is at least evidence of how the first lines of Shakespeare's first sonnet were read by one of their first readers because one could not arrive at such capitalization and italicization *without* reading for proper names.

"Rose" was also associated in early modern England (as it probably still is today, as in expressions like "The Rose of Tralee") with specifically *female* beauty. "Creatures" in the first line is so general as to allow for the possibility of plant cultivation and animal husbandry as much as the propagation of human life, thus: the origin of and instigation for ("desire") the arts of cultivation and propagation of species arises from beauty ("From fairest"). For aesthetic reasons, it is especially significant that it is not the other way round – that is to say, art neither generates nor precedes beauty, but, crucially, derives from it. In both humans and animals (though not in plants), the feminine is the vehicle of this increase; that is, new members of the species must be born of the mother. This is so obvious it seems spurious; but the logic of this sonnet is such as to suggest that the young man has at his command the power to reproduce himself all on his own, without benefit of a female partner, if he would but set his mind to it. In those sonnets where there is a reference to the mother of the youth's offspring, she is not so much a person as a thing, an "uneared [not yet fruitful] womb" (Sonnet 3.5), or an incidental afterthought, "some mother" (3.4). There is no argument in these poems that the young man should marry anyone in particular, which is all the more astonishing since the argument for marriage here is precisely that he should marry *now*. Nor is there any sense that the youth should fall in love with a woman. On the contrary, he is enjoined to cut to the chase and get on with the essential business of duplicating himself.

Despite his earlier opposition to matrimony, Southampton finally married a woman he had already impregnated, the ravishing beauty Lady Elizabeth Vernon. A surviving portrait shows her posed as Venus, in a bejeweled open gown, her long hair falling in waves around her shoulders, one enormous pearl-drop earring visible amid her ample tresses, her hand placed over her right breast whose nipple is barely covered by her open bodice. Contra Shakespeare's *Venus and Adonis*, written for Southampton, where Adonis is a reluctant youth who is simply not attracted to the divine embodiment of female beauty, the goddess of love, the painting seems to say Southampton's Venus has now married him. Further, the gesture toward the breast is a sign of bounty and fecundity, and while these are conventions of artistic representation at the time, this extraordinarily sensuous portrait of a wife was relatively unusual in the representation of dynastic marriages.

While Southampton was in possession of an earldom, he married for love rather than money as his wife was the daughter of a country squire and only in court circles at all because of a familial tie to the Earl of Essex, who provided her with a meager annual income of £50. This is not to make a claim for Southampton as the addressee of the sonnets, but it is a historical reminder that "From fairest creatures we desire increase / That thereby beauty's *Rose* might never die" reads differently if understood as addressed to *male* readers – and the majority of readers in early modern England *were* male. As an address to a male audience, these first two lines taken in isolation could be understood as referring to the process of selecting a wife. There was certainly ample precedent in the sonnet tradition for an address to a male audience who can be assumed to share a particular mindset. For example, Sir Thomas Wyatt's translation of Petrarch's *Candida Cerva* is the angry and frustrated sonnet, "Whoso list to hunt, I know where is an hind" that translates to something like the collusive misogyny of "I know a girl who puts out." The tone of Shakespeare's opening lines is far more relaxed, but *"Rose"* supports the reading that what is at issue here is the search for a female sexual object, because it was a common euphemism for female genitalia.

Shakespeare was undoubtedly familiar with the Dutch humanist scholar Erasmus's "Epistle to persuade a young gentleman to marriage," because it had been translated into English as an example of the art of persuasive rhetoric in Thomas Wilson's *The Art of Rhetorique* (1553). Erasmus, like the speaker of the sonnets, does not trouble himself even to mention the name of the bride he has in mind for his young friend as he exhorts him to wedlock:

> There was at supper with me the twelfth day of April, when I lay in the country, Antonius Baldus, a man (as you know) that most earnestly tendereth your welfare, and one that hath been always of great acquaintance, and familiarity with your son-in-law: a heavy feast we had, and full of much mourning. He told me greatly to both our heaviness, that your mother that most godly woman, was departed this life, and your sister being overcome with sorrow and heaviness, had made her self a nun, so that in you only remaineth the hope of issue [offspring], and maintenance of your stock. Whereupon your friends with one consent, have offered you in marriage, a gentlewoman of a good house, and much wealth, faire of body, very well brought up, and such a one as loveth you with all her heart. But you (either for your late sorrows, which you have in fresh remembrance, or else for religion's sake) have so purposed to live a single life, that neither can you for love of your stock, neither for desire of issue, nor yet for any entreaty of your friends can make, either by praying, or by weeping: be brought to change your mind. And yet notwithstanding all this (if you will follow my counsel) you shall be of an other mind, and leaving to live single, which both is barren, and smally [little] agreeing with the state of man's nature, you shall give your self wholly to most holy wedlock. And for this part, I will neither wish, that the love of your friends (which else ought to overcome your nature) nor yet mine authority that I have over you, should do me any good at all, to compass this my request, if I shall not prove unto you by most plain reasons, that it will be both much more honest, more profitable, and also most pleasant for you to marry, than to live otherwise. (Wilson, 74, 152)

Not only, however, does Erasmus's general argument comport with that of the first seventeen sonnets, but so also do the numerous analogies between the propagation of plant species and the propagation of the human species. In one remarkable section entitled "Marriage among Trees," using the classical writer Pliny as his source, Erasmus makes the argument (in astonishingly anthropomorphizing terms) that everything in creation has an innate propensity to reproduce itself:

> I will not speak now of Trees, wherein (as Pliny most certainly writeth) there is found marriage, with some manifest difference of both kinds, that except the husband tree, do lean with his boughs, even as though he should desire copulation upon the women Trees, growing round about him: They would else altogether wax barren. The same Pliny also doeth report, that certain authors do think there is both male and female in all things that the earth yieldeth.

What is astonishing here is the putative heterosexuality of absolutely everything in the natural order. In the first sonnet, this sense of following nature's alleged prescription is somewhat overshadowed by the inexplicable over-investment the poet has in the young man's sexual life. Further, it is not, as the reader is first led to expect, the young man's potential female partner who is the fairest creature alluded to in the first line but the young man himself, who is, the poem tells us, *"the only"* augurer of spring (line 10) – a description which precludes any female contenders for the title of fairest creature:

> From fairest creatures we desire increase,
> That thereby beauty's *Rose* might never die,
> But as the riper should by time decease,
> His tender heir might bear his memory:
> But thou contracted to thine own bright eyes,
> Feed'st thy light's flame with self-substantial fuel,
> Making a famine where abundance lies,
> Thy self thy foe, to thy sweet self too cruel:
> Thou that art now the world's fresh ornament,
> And only herald to the gaudy spring,
> Within thine own bud buryest thy content,
> And, tender churl, mak'st waste in niggarding:
>   Pity the world, or else this glutton be,
>   To eat the world's due, by the grave and thee.
>
> (Sonnet 1)

For the poet does not go on after the first two lines simply to encourage the young man to marry, but rather proceeds to accuse him of all manner of related crimes in refusing to do so. The only intimation of the nature of the marriage the poet envisages for the young man is in the word "contracted," which implies the marriage contract the youth rejects, as well as the contractual arrangements of dowry and betrothal. Additionally, contracted connotes the process of legal containment.

There is certainly the sense that in his single state the youth restricts rather than expands his potential, which is of course the theme of Ovid's Narcissus who, falling in love with his image in the water, falls in and drowns as he seeks to embrace it. The poet accuses the young man of narcissism (line 5), of waste and masturbatory self-indulgence (line 6), of the artificial creation of dearth (line 7), of gluttony (line 13), and he makes good on the threat in the final couplet with the promise of death. This sonnet is not a love poem, and it sounds, at least from one perspective, like the poet is advocating a lucrative match. A further possible interpretation of the opening sestet, then, is that the real problem is that the youth refuses to marry *to financial advantage*. From this point of view it is rather like advice given to Robert Cecil by his father, Lord Burghley: "Let her [your bride] not be poor, how generous [nobly born] so ever [she may be] . . . Gentility is nothing but ancient riches" (Akrigg, 40). Critics have argued that the pervasive financial imagery of the sonnets – here registered as "waste" (profligacy), "niggarding" (hoarding), etc. – is indicative of the new, emergent economic system of capitalism. However, in Shakespeare's appropriation of the aristocratic genre of the sonnet there remains visible the incorporation within this new economic system of the much older practice of making dynastic marriages for money. This was, after all, a business over which William Cecil, Lord Burghley, held total control as Master of the Court of Wards under Elizabeth, which was essentially a clearing house for the marriageable offspring of the landed classes.

Also embedded within the first sonnet, and indeed within the sequence as a whole, is the profoundly Ovidian theme of the inevitability of change, in the face of which resistance is nothing less than the choice of death over life. "Rose," "ripe," "tender," and "bud" all indicate vegetative life, and it is, of course, this condition – the complete attenuation and loss of human identity – that befalls many mortals who in some way or other thwart the cruel and capricious wills of deities in Ovid's *Metamorphoses*. For example, pursued by Jove in Book 2, Daphne prays for the earth to swallow her, and it obliges, allowing her to reemerge as a laurel tree. In Book 10, Myrrah, who refuses Cupid's advances, finds herself giving birth to Adonis from the bark (literally, in Latin, the rind) of a myrrh tree. Shakespeare, however, also reverses this Ovidian trajectory, so that the young man *begins* life as already a bud, "only herald of the gaudy spring," who may no longer have the prospect of ripening ("riper," line 3). By the end of the poem, what awaits the failure to reproduce is much worse than Ovidian transformation back into the fertile compost heap of organic matter; it is the absolute negation of life as opposed to life transposed to a lower register, or life lived in another form.

It is not impossible that Shakespeare was commissioned by Burghley to write the first seventeen sonnets to one of his recalcitrant wards, and we would do well to remember Jonathan Bate's caution that "Shakespeare was not a Romantic poet who just sat down and wrote a sonnet when he felt one coming on" (Bate, 38). What remains confounding, however, even if we accept the notion that Shakespeare was writing on commission, is the way that these poems so far exceed their brief. Of course, if Shakespeare set out to persuade someone to marry we might reasonably expect he might indeed do it much better than we could imagine. But even genius cannot account for the intimacy of the petition, the sheer emotional insistence with which the first seventeen poems make their demand. They do not seem to do so at the behest of some social superior such as Burghley, but entirely on the poet's own behalf. The early sonnets want the young man's child, his copy in the world with an urgency of desire that is almost unfathomable. Indeed, there are moments when the poet seems to want the young man, impossibly, to have *his* child: "Make thee another self for love of me" (Sonnet 10.13). Desire of course always exceeds demand: "Childhood love," writes Freud, "is boundless . . . it demands exclusive possession, it is not content with less than all. But it has a second characteristic: it has, in point of fact, no aim and is incapable of obtaining complete satisfaction; and principally for that reason it is doomed to end in disappointment" (quoted Phillips, 39). In other words, love without an explicitly erotic aim, if that is indeed the story of the young man sonnets, would effect an interesting twist on the unavailability of the love object in the Petrarchan tradition.

The erasure of women and women's bodies that would be required in order that the young man reproduce is striking in the first seventeen sonnets: "Thou dost beguile the world, unbless some mother. / For where is she so fair whose uneared womb / Distains the tillage of thy husbandry" (Sonnet 3.4–6). Yet, the lineage suggested in this sonnet is entirely a maternal one: "Thou art thy mother's glass, and she in thee / Calls back the lovely April of their prime" (3.9–10). Here, the young man is, oddly, the beautiful image of his mother – not his father – and yet in this erratic scheme of lineage and heredity the young man's child will bear his image, not that of the child's mother. This is a strange patriarchy, a new model of reproduction, which requires not so much the erasure as the appropriation of femininity so as to allow Shakespeare to co-opt the more traditional associations of beauty with femininity. Thus, femininity in the poem resides not only in nature, and in the youth's mother, but also, crucially, in the young man whom the poet endows with a distinctly female capacity for generation.

In Sonnet 20 the connection between beauty and femininity becomes explicit as the poet makes the intriguing case that the young man is a physically and morally superior species of woman. The poem, like so many of the stories in Ovid's *Metamorphoses*, is a myth about the origins of the young man and of how he came to possess such extraordinary beauty. In Sonnet 20 nature somewhat resembles Aristotle's view, widely promulgated in the Renaissance, that nature strove toward perfection and, of course, that perfection was male. In order to help nature along during the reproductive act, Artistotle suggested tying the left testicle with a strong piece of rope (the left or "sinister" side was associated with femininity: it is not known if this practice was widely attempted). Nature's means of striving for perfection in the sonnet are considerably less painful. However, enamored of her creative process, like an artist who cannot bring herself to leave well enough alone, nature continues to work on "painting" the young man, until she has added the ostensibly extraneous "thing," the feminine young man's penis:

> A woman's face with nature's own hand painted,
> Hast thou the master mistress of my passion,
> A woman's gentle heart but not acquainted
> With shifting change as is false women's fashion,
> An eye more bright than theirs, less false in rolling:

Importantly here, the literary object used to represent the young man – that is, the sonnet – is itself feminine, containing wholly feminine rhymes. That is, the lines are all hypermetrical because there is an additional unstressed syllable at the end. Like nature, the feminine force that has fashioned the young man in the first place, in the poet's lyrical refashioning of his beauty he has added "one thing" to every line, that extra syllable which does not serve the purposes of a masculine ending:

> And for a woman wert thou first created,
> Till nature as she wrought thee fell a-doting,
> And by addition me of thee defeated,
> By adding one thing to my purpose nothing.

There are echoes of Christopher Marlowe's epyllion or "feminine" epic, *Hero and Leander*, in Shakespeare's descriptions of beauty in the sonnets. In Marlowe's poem nature, also, following convention, personified as female, worries that she has so generously bestowed her gifts on the divine Hero that she is now herself in deficit:

> So lovely fair was Hero . . .
> As Nature wept, thinking she was undone;
> Because she took more from her than she left,
> And of such wondrous beauty her bereft:
> Therefore in sign her treasure suffered wrack,
> Since Hero's time, hath half the world been black
> (*Hero and Leander*, 45–51)

These are strikingly similar themes to those pursued in the sonnets: beauty has become scarce because nature lavished so much of it on Hero that there is not enough left to bestow on anyone else. The symptom of this deficit is that half the world is now black. Similarly, the "black beauty" of the sonnets addressed to the "woman colored ill," as we shall discuss shortly, is the aesthetic detritus of the unimpeachable beauty of the young man.

The young man resembles the ambivalent identity of the figure of Hermaphroditus, the fair youth pursued by the nymph Salmacis whose sexual advances – shades of the youth's reluctance to marry – he repulses in Book 4 of the *Metamorphoses*. As Hermaphroditus tries to escape the nymph, he jumps into a pond:

> The nymph to have her hoped sport: she urges him likewise.
> And pressing him with all her might, fast cleaving to him still,

Strive, struggle, wrest and writhe (she said) thou forward [obstinate]
   boy thy fill:
Doe what thou canst thou shalt not scape. The gods of heaven agree
That this same willful boy and I may never parted be.
The gods were pliant to her boon [request]. The bodies of them twain
Were mixed and joined both in one. To both them did remain
One countenance: . . .
                Through her hugging and her grasping of the other
The members of them mingled were and fastened both together,
They were not any longer two: but (as it were) a toy
Of double shape. **You could not say it was a perfect boy**
Nor perfect wench: it seemed both and none of both to be.
                           (Golding IV.457–70, my emphasis)

"One thing to my purpose nothing" is a joke on genitalia. "Thing" is slang for penis, and as readers of *Hamlet* know all too well, Ophelia's "Nothing my lord" is taken by the Prince of Denmark to mean "country [cunt-ry] matters," in other words, as a reference to the female orifice. The young man has a woman's heart, that is, a feminine essence, but none of the innate moral frailties typically attributed in this period to the "daughters of Eve." The young man is "not acquainted" with the transgressions typical of women (changeableness and false, "rolling [roving]" eyes). However, the "quaint" of "acquainted" is in early modern pronunciation homonymic with "cunt," so the double entendre of the line is that the young man has a woman's heart but not her pudenda. This sonnet has famously been used to argue *both* that Shakespeare had specifically sexual longings for the young man *and* that he did not. The poem does not tell us whether the poet consummated his relationship with the young man, and indeed the poem cannot of itself resolve the issue of Shakespeare's sexual identity, but it leaves us in no doubt that the poet does in this poem express sexual longing for him. The poem plays with the reader in terms of whether we read the young man's masculinity as an obstacle to that consummation or as simply a more alluring inducement to it.

The young man is, as line 7 states, a man whose external parts, his "hue," compel desire and admiration from all quarters regardless of gender, or for that matter sexual predilection. Alternatively, he is a man possessed of a malleable beauty that presents itself as both male and female: "A man in hue, all hues in his controlling."[1] Hue in the sense of color might also refer to facial color (pallor or blushing), which is the sense of the word as it is used in Sonnet 82, a poem about the garish ways in which the rival poets have depicted the young man: "Thou art as fair in knowledge as in hue" (82.5). Here the rival poets are conceived like nature, as painters, but they are simply bad artists whose "gross painting" (82.13) mars what it strives to depict. In both Sonnets 20 and 82, the fair youth is not just beautiful, he *is* a work of art.

Despite, then, the enormous critical energy that has been expended on the first lines of Sonnet 20 – "A woman's face with nature's own hand painted, / Hast thou the master mistress of my passion" – the focus on enigmatic sexuality and ambiguous sexual identity has perhaps obscured a more overarching point about the relation between beauty and the art it inspires. As the poet's Muse, the young man would be the mistress of the poet's creative capacities, whereas as the poet's patron or social superior, he would be the master.

Although we do not know whether Sonnet 20 was composed before or after *Hero and Leander* (1593), Marlowe also focuses primarily on Leander's masculine beauty (his descriptions of Hero's beauty are largely confined to her clothes):

> . . . my slack muse, sings of Leander's eyes,
> Those orient cheeks and lips, exceeding his
> That lept into the water for a kiss
> Of his own shadow, and despising many,
> Died ere he could enjoy the love of any. . . .
> Some swore he was a maid in mans attire,
> For in his looks were all that men desire
> (*Hero and Leander*, 72–84ff.)

Like Shakespeare's young man, Leander is as beautiful as Narcissus, who presumably would not have fallen in love with himself if he had not been already sexually inclined toward men. Shakespeare's young man, also associated with Narcissus, is identified throughout the sequence as Helen of Troy, the mythic paradigm of female beauty. Furthermore, the references to the young man as Helen are references not only to an orthodox standard of beauty, but also to a model of female beauty that is coterminous with its artistic representation:

> Describe Adonis, and the counterfeit
> Is poorly imitated after you;

On Helen's cheek all art of beauty set,
And you in Grecian tires [attire] are painted new
(Sonnet 53)

Interestingly in Sonnet 53, all representations of the addressee are not equal. Adonis is a poor imitation of the beloved, whereas Helen's face – cosmeticized either by herself or by the artist who painted her and her garments – appears to be satisfactory: "you in Grecian tires are painted new." However, this positive appraisal is qualified by the sense that this is only a good likeness of the beloved if the painting is perfectly executed, with consummate skill, *only if* there is on Helen's face in the painting "all art of beauty set." Of course the young man is never described with any physiognomic specificity; we do not even access the characteristics of his beauty via the litany of Petrarchan metaphor. The poet's goal is not the specificity of portraiture, but precisely the non-specificity that allows for the articulation of ideal beauty.

Sonnet 18, "Shall I compare thee to a summer's day?" – arguably the most well-loved poem in the English language – seems to suspend, at least temporarily, the controversies that have raged about the identity of the persons to whom the sonnets are addressed in favor of extolling the beauty of the poet's beloved. In this poem, the only gendered pronoun refers not to its addressee but to death. Reading the 1609 Quarto sequentially, the context of this poem is the series of urgent addresses to the young man that have preceded it. This sonnet uses conventional images of natural beauty to demonstrate that the beauty of the beloved surpasses even the most sublime of these, and further, that only poetry is capable of capturing and sustaining the addressee's beauty. For even the youth's beauty is, like all other worldly things, subject to the depredations of time. This exquisite lyric is, of course, about the young man, but it is also (like Sonnet 130, "My mistress' eyes are nothing like the sun") about the limits of poetic language – of conventional poetic metaphor and simile in particular – to image the loveliness of the youth. Poetry not only gives life to the young man, it also bestows upon him an enhanced and intensified life, as he is spared from death by the breath and the sight of readers as they enunciate the verse or see it on the page: "So long as men can breathe, or eyes can see, / So long lives this, and this gives life to thee" (18.13–14). Life and beauty may be fleeting, but the poet promises them for eternity, and he promises them via specifically literary means.

Breath is after all the stuff of language, and the metrical organization of a poem controls and patterns the breath; sight, on the other hand, is the material dimension of the printed or written word. The longevity of breath and sight assures the enunciation and reading of poetry. Indeed, Shakespeare's meditations on the relation between beauty in life and beauty in art – the "art of beauty," the "painted counterfeit" – suggest the powerful possibility and power of representing, replicating, and preserving physical beauty both in poetry ("my pupil pen," "a modern quill," 83.7) and in the visual arts ("pencil," a fine portrait brush, 16).

"Shall I compare thee to a summer's day," then, follows hard upon the heels of the first seventeen poems of the sequence, which far from following the traditional rubric of Petrarchanism prosecute the extraordinary argument that the heedless youth will fail as a custodian of his own beauty if he does not marry and reproduce. In Sonnet 18, the only lingering notion of this resides in the sense that his life potential might be abruptly curtailed at any moment. In a world where a significant proportion of humanity failed to survive even into adulthood and where diseases like smallpox could ravage beauty at any moment (as it did to any number of people, including Queen Elizabeth herself, who contracted smallpox in 1563), there was perhaps a heightened consciousness of the omnipresence of death even where life seemed at its most vigorous and intense.

The young man sonnets, then, offer a meditation on physical, embodied male beauty as both the inspiration and the aesthetic end of poetry itself. Beauty thus instigates both biological reproduction and artistic imitation. Living, breathing beauty is the only kind that deserves the name, and it must be imitated by an art capable of endowing these animating qualities, by verse that "gives life" (Sonnet 18.14). The inert facsimile of beauty represented by cosmetics, and by bad art, on the other hand, especially the art of rival poets, is not beauty at all.

Black Beauty

Shakespeare refers to the woman romantically referred to since the nineteenth century as the "dark lady" as "black." Editors and critics have been at pains to tell readers that this probably does not mean that the "woman colored ill" "whose breasts are dun" (Sonnet 130) is actually an African or person of African descent, but that she is more likely a raven-haired but white-skinned beauty. However, in the absence of evidence, we must admit the possibility, especially since there were Africans in England at this time, that the woman Shakespeare or his imaginative alter ego both loved and reviled was actually black. Further, Shakespeare was sufficiently interested in racial difference to write about it repeatedly in his career, in *The Merchant of Venice*, *Titus Andronicus*, as well as *Othello*. Critics have claimed that the sonnets addressed to the woman colored ill are among the earliest, and certainly, as we have seen in chapter 1, Sonnet 145 certainly fits that category. Additionally, 138 and 144 appear in *The Passionate Pilgrim* of 1599, and these poems do not represent the rich and unusual vocabulary that we associate with Shakespeare's writing after the turn of the century. For all that, the theme of black versus white, as a visual distinction, a philosophical antithesis, and a racial phenomenon, is so much at the heart of Shakespeare's Jacobean tragedy *Othello* that it seems unlikely that all of the "dark lady" poems are early compositions, and if they are, they may well have been ones that he revisited shortly before their publication in 1609. In that play too, he imagines the creative work of the African woman that has gone into making the handkerchief Othello's mother gave him and that in turn he presented to Desdemona as his first love token. The "prophetic fury" with which this woman sews is analogous to poetic frenzy, and one suspects that Shakespeare may be projecting some of his own more exalted imaginative moments onto this figure. In the sonnets in contrast, there is no positive perspective to be had on the woman. Katherine Duncan-Jones has described these poems as outrageously misogynist and underlines "the sheer nastiness of many of the 'dark lady' sonnets, which can now be seen to encompass not so much passionate devotion to a distantly cruel mistress as an elaborate mockery of a woman who is no more than a sexual convenience" (Duncan-Jones, 1997, 51).

The model for the sonnet lady was of course Petrarch's Laura, who is fair and beautiful beyond compare, but chaste, cold, and distant. On account of this distance, and because in the Petrarchan tradition the lady cruelly refuses to relent and show mercy on her admirer, there is an inherent antagonism between the lover-poet and the lady who endangers his very survival and has utterly destroyed his emotional world. In *Romeo and Juliet*, Shakespeare dramatized this idea and took the notion of the lover as "loathed enemy" into the arena of social conflict. In this play, the lovers are literally enemies because they belong to feuding families: Juliet to the Capulets and Romeo to the Montagues. The sonnets pursue this idea in a different direction. The dark mistress elaborates the idea of the woman as enemy, but instead of being physically distant and chaste, refusing to consummate the poet-lover's desires, she and the poet are physically intimate and she is promiscuous: her vagina is described in Sonnet 137 as "the bay where all men ride" (line 6). In Petrarch, love enters by the eyes, "the doors and hallways of tears," but in Shakespeare the eyes become unreliable monitors of beauty because the poet's sexual entanglement has mesmerized and deluded him to the point where his eyes "know what beauty is, see where it lies, / Yet what the best is, take the worst to be" (137.2–3).

Of the twenty-eight sonnets addressing the woman, the vast majority recount her vile and contemptible moral nature rather than her unconventional physical attractions. The first two sonnets of those addressed to the mistress are by far the most benign. The first treats the uniqueness of her idiosyncratic, dusky beauty, and the second, her musical skills. Notably, the emphasis in the sonnets to the female addressee is not on the replication of her image but on the question of the possible justification for her admission to the precincts of beauty. The first sonnet in this section, 127, also picks up the theme of the association of "painting," that is, cosmetics with bad art that we saw in Sonnet 82. The poet refers to the changing tastes dating from the 1590s when blackness became the object of cultural fascination shared by many of his contemporaries, a taste that already had a biblical precedent in the *Song of Solomon*: "I am black, but comely" (1.4). Richard Barnfield, whose homoerotic sequence of twenty sonnets addressed to Ganymede in *Cynthia* (1595) may have influenced Shakespeare's young man poems, had urged elsewhere that "white compared to black is much condemned." In the 1601 edition of Samual Daniel's sonnet sequence *Delia*, Delia is presented as a raven-haired beauty, and even the alabaster white Stella of Sidney's sequence had black eyes. A further indication that there was a new interest in the black dimensions of beauty is that James I's wife Queen Anne commissioned Ben Jonson to write *The Masque of Blackness* in which she and her retinue of court ladies would appear as "blackamoors." In

Love's Labours Lost (1595–6) 4.3.245–9, the courtier Berowne falls in love with the dark-complexioned Rosaline, which allows him to engage in some rhetorical acrobatics to reconfigure cultural stereotypes around beauty and whiteness:

> Is ebony like her? O word divine!
> A wife of such wood were felicity.
> O, who can give an oath? where is a book?
> That I may swear beauty doth beauty lack,
> If that she learn not of her eye to look:
> No face is fair that is not full so black!

The desire to swear that black is beautiful is reminiscent of the poet's oath of Sonnet 132, "I swear beauty herself is black" (line 13), and of the disillusioned speaker's recollection in Sonnet 147 that "I have sworn thee fair" (line 13). Berowne's oath too argues that, as it is conventionally understood as bright/blonde, beauty is in fact deficient, and what it lacks is blackness. Berowne's opinion, not surprisingly, is of the minority:

> O paradox! Black is the badge of hell,
> The hue of dungeons and the school of night
> (*Love's Labours Lost*, 4.3.250–1)

While "the school of night" referred to the occult interests of Sir Walter Ralegh and his circle, it also connotes the more obvious associations of night with sexual congress, and with literally the underside of female beauty, the hidden genital orifice. In the sonnets, Shakespeare explores both the paradox of black beauty and the notion that black is the badge of hell, with whose infernal regions the woman is repeatedly associated: "Who art as black as hell, and dark as night" (147.14); "none knows well / To shun the heaven that leads men to this hell" (129.13–14).

Further, black beauty is a paradox in early modern society, which was entering into much greater contact with the wider world, and part of the discovery entailed in such encounters was the lure of otherness, the sometimes fearful fascination that arises in encountering cultural and physiological differences. As we have noted, Shakespeare was still preoccupied by the stark contrast between black and white beauty into the seventeenth century. He does not, of course, represent the black general, Othello, as beautiful, any more than he represents Macbeth or Lear as physically superior physical specimens. Rather, he is concerned here with how Desdemona, alabaster white in both appearance and morality, can be taken as black; and how Bianca, whose name means white, can be a prostitute whose moral sense extends beyond the narrow confines of the chastity she does not possess. In Act 2.1, the arch-villain Iago banters about the relation between women's complexion and their virtue:

> *Iago*: If she be fair and wise, fairness and wit;
>   The one's for use, the other using it.
> *Desdemona*: Well prais'd! How if she be black and witty?
> *Iago*: If she be black, and thereto have a wit,
>   She'll find a white, that shall her blackness hit.
> <div align="right">(<i>Othello</i>, 2.1.129–33)</div>

This passage provides an important parallel to the sonnets because the conversation is not specifically about African women, but about dark women of European origin. However, in the context of the play, these remarks clearly extend to African women, and to racial difference itself. Here, Shakespeare works over again some of the central themes of the sonnets: the relations between being fair and the sexual sense of "use" in Sonnet 20's "mine be thy use." In Iago's jest, fair woman is to manipulate her sexuality, her "fair" appearance, according to her wit. The suggestion here, unlike in the young man sonnets, is something like manipulation, or in modern terms, sleeping your way to the top. According to Iago, if the woman is black and "witty," that is, sexually knowing or shrewd, she will find a man (a "white") who will have sex with her, "that shall her blackness hit."

Of course golden hair and a fair complexion were the features praised in the Petrarchan blazon, the lyrical itinerary of female beauty. The poet, therefore, is not merely claiming beauty for someone who is "black" but simultaneously creating an aesthetic contrary to the orthodoxies of the genre in which he is writing. That Shakespeare's interest in what we might call "black aesthetics" in the sonnets is not an isolated phenomenon – either in his own work or in that of his culture more generally – does not however mean that it is *only* an aesthetic phenomenon:

In the old age black was not counted fair,
Or if it were it bore not beauty's name:
But now is black beauty's successive heir,
And beauty slandered with a bastard shame,
For since each hand hath put on nature's power,
Fairing the foul with art's false borrowed face,
Sweet beauty hath no name, no holy bower,
But is profaned, if not lives in disgrace.
Therefore my mistress' eyes are raven black,
Her eyes so suited, and they mourners seem,
At such who not born fair no beauty lack,
Slandering creation with a false esteem,
  Yet so they mourn becoming of their woe,
  That every tongue says beauty should look so.

(Sonnet 127)

Following directly from Sonnet 126's address to the unproblematically "lovely boy" (126.1), in 127 the "old age" or golden age of antiquity now long passed has been experienced by the reader in just the preceding poem. This sonnet is quite literally, that is, in terms of the order of the sonnets in the Quarto, "beauty's successive heir." Black's inheritance must be legitimate because illegitimate scions of the nobility were barred from inheriting titles. Even so, the poem tells us, because the heir of beauty is black, people falsely say that this black child of beauty is a "bastard" (line 4). Rhetorically, this is a clever argument, even though it is a biologically implausible one.

The poem not only defends the inherent beauty of blackness, however; it also taps into one of the most common themes of misogynist discourse in the period, namely the argument against cosmetics, intimations of which are apparent also, as we have seen, in Sonnet 20's "A woman's face with nature's own hand painted." Hamlet too condemns the cosmetic impersonation of beauty: "The harlot's cheek beautied with plast'ring art" (3.1.51). What was "plastered" on was a fairly lethal concoction of white lead and egg white, enhanced with rouged cheeks and lips. Not only was this image of beauty – golden hair, lily white skin, teeth like pearls, cheeks like roses, and lips like coral – the dominant one in the cultural consciousness of medieval and Renaissance Europe, it was also the very model of beauty promulgated by the sonnet tradition. Shakespeare thus takes issue with sonnet convention from the very first sonnet in the Quarto addressed to a woman. Cosmetics, like the garish rhetoric employed by the rival poets in Sonnet 82 to depict the young man, are mere artifice, and when actual cosmetics are used by women, it is outright misrepresentation, the appearance and not the reality of beauty. Thus the alliterations in "Fairing the foul with art's false borrowed face" work to reflect in language the unnatural effects that the poet is condemning. Women who use cosmetics usurp the work of nature, so that sacred beauty is profaned and has no place to go. The darkness of the mistress becomes an indictment of those who use cosmetics. Indeed, the mistress's raven-black eyes are mourners who figure an elegiac lament for the demise of unadulterated beauty. The paradox of the final couplet is that this funereal blackness becomes the very paradigm of beauty.

In aesthetic terms, the rhetoric of Petrarchanism was antiquated by the time it flowered in English poetry in the sixteenth century. Yet poets still persisted in the hackneyed phrases to describe women's beauty. Here, for example, is part of Henry Constable's sonnet, which describes those physical attributes that make the lady delectably kissable:

> . . . thy hand is soft is sweet is white
> Thy lips sweet roses, breast sweet lily is
> That love esteems these three the chiefest bliss
> Which nature ever made for lips's delight

Compared with the cloying sweetness of Constable's lyric, there is something refreshingly caustic about Shakespeare's Sonnet 130:

> My mistress' eyes are nothing like the sun,
> Coral is far more red, than her lips red,
> If snow be white, why then her breasts are dun:
> If hairs be wires, black wires grow on her head:
> I have seen roses damasked, red and white,
> But no such roses see I in her cheeks,
> And in some perfumes is there more delight,
> Than in the breath that from my mistress reeks.
> I love to hear her speak, yet well I know,
> That music hath a far more pleasing sound:
> I grant I never saw a goddess go,
> My mistress when she walks treads on the ground.

And yet by heaven I think my love as rare,
As any she belied with false compare.

(Sonnet 130)

Shakespeare here counters a fourteenth-century Petrarchan tradition that lauded the aristocratic and unavailable mistress in a social context that did not give women power – even the most elite of them – despite, or perhaps because of, its elevation of the feminine ideal. In the Petrarchan blazon, the conventional poetic catalog extolling the beauty of the beloved's various anatomical features – eye, hand, brow, etc. – referred to in Sonnet 106 as "the blazon of sweet beauty's best" (106.5), the lyrical objectives are idealization and praise.

The emphasis from the very start of 130 is on specificity, "*My* mistress" (130.1, 130.12) The first line is a bold contradiction of Petrarchan precedent. The sonnet moves from colors, red, white, black, and from red and white to roses, and from roses to perfume, to breath, from goddess to heaven. In the course of a single lyric, Shakespeare rehearses what is essentially the very core of issues about the nature of poetic language, which must be sufficiently recognizable as the stuff of everyday life to move the reader, and yet sufficiently elevated from the language of everyday life to constitute poetry.

Nor should we think of the Petrarchan blazon as simply idealizing and its Shakespearean reversal as simply misogynist. In fact, there was a kind of violent anatomical dissection at play in many poems of the Petrarchan tradition as the mistress was broken down into discrete body parts to be itemized by her male appraiser. Petrarchanism, in fact, worked to efface female subjectivity and to reduce the woman to little more than the objects to which she was compared. By the time of the English sonnet craze, some of these comparisons are already mildly risible: Sir Walter Ralegh describes his mistress as having "lips of jelly," "violet breath," "eyes of light," while Spenser's fiancée has nipples like jasmines and breasts like young does.[2] The latter image, bizarre as it might seem, actually originates from an even earlier text, the *Song of Solomon*: "Thy lips are like a thread of scarlet . . . Thy two breasts are like two young roes that are twins, which feed among the lilies" (4.3–5). Thus the language of idealized female beauty is ancient, and familiar to the point of being hackneyed.

Although in *Hero and Leander* Marlowe reserves his genuinely sensual description for "Leander, beautiful and young," Hero is playfully described as having hands "so white" that the sun and wind refuse to burn or chafe them, while her breath is so beautifully perfumed that it attracts bees who take it for the odor of honeysuckle:

> Many would praise the sweet smell as she past,
> When t'was the odor which her breath forth cast.
> And there for honey, bees have sought in vain,
> And beat from thence, have lighted there againe.
> (*Hero and Leander*, 21–4)

At first glance, the poet in the sonnets may seem to be taking issue with precisely such idealized descriptions in the lines, "And in some perfumes is there more delight, / Than in the breath that from my mistress reeks." On closer examination, however, the sonnet may share the mockingly humorous tone of Marlowe's poem, where Hero's breath smells so good that she attracts stinging insects.

In Sonnet 130, Shakespeare places innovative pressure upon the limits of metaphoricity. Further, this sonnet interrogates the notion of a causal or necessary relationship between ideal female beauty and male desire and instead presents the radical idea that there may be a disjunction between them. The point of the poem is not only that this particular woman does not meet the ideal standard of blonde Petrarchan beauty, but that no woman does. Even the fairest woman is possessed, as Iago remarked, of that vaginal darkness, the shadow of idealized female beauty, which Petrarchan rhetoric does not need to incorporate. Thus the poet is unable in the "dark lady" sonnets to defend against accusations about lyrical misrepresentation that he readily dispatched in earlier descriptions of the fair young man when he addressed the charge that: "this poet lies, / Such heavenly touches ne'er touched earthly faces" (17.7–8).

Poetry's detractors in this period were fond of opining that all literature was inherently deceptive because it was the work of the imagination. The sonnets engage with this charge obliquely, arguing that the tropes of lyrical beauty are insufficiently idealized in relation to glorious masculine beauty, and over-idealized in relation to the beauty of women. What the poet has to say about his mistress in Sonnet 130 extends to all women: "any she belied with false compare" (130.14). Petrarchan love, of course, was love at a long distance. Distance fosters idealization in a way that familiarity and intimacy do not. Sonnet 130 deliberately disengages with the lyrical tradition, gesturing toward its inability to represent femininity in a way that is not always already aestheticized. The unpoetic oath, "by heaven," effects a shift from the lyrical to the colloquial register in order to demonstrate that even goddesses are overrated.

*

Petrarchanism was the European code of lyrical beauty, as Gary Waller puts it, "the inevitable language in which the poet and lover alike necessarily had to struggle" (Waller, 77). We return then to the way in which lyric inevitably straddles the issue of representing love and the experience of love itself.

CHAPTER 4

Love

Love in its ideal form, where there is no sense of discord between the poet and his love object, first presents itself in Sonnet 18, "Shall I compare thee to a summer's day." Offering a brief respite from the threats and accusations that have characterized the first seventeen sonnets, this sonnet rests, albeit briefly, undisturbed by such roil and tumult, in appreciation of the youth's beauty. Sonnet 18 thus conforms to the devotion popularly expected of a love sonnet. The poet's faith in the youth will be shattered in subsequent sonnets by grief, agitation, anxiety, and betrayal. Yet, even here, in the tranquil equilibrium of Sonnet 18, there are intimations of the inclement emotional climate that will soon perturb him: "rough winds," intense heat ("sometimes too hot the eye of heaven shines"), unhappy or even tragic accidents ("chance"), or perhaps just the process of attrition that belongs to life itself, the inherent obsolescence of organic matter. Such threats to the inherently fragile beauty of a life just beginning to bloom constitute the poet's fears about losing love, and even his adoring idealization cannot fully excise or assuage them. The final couplet, however, offers more optimism than the majority of the sonnets about the capacity of poetry to make love and the beloved immortal.

Of course, as Shakespeare himself observed, "The course of true love never did run smooth" (*A Midsummer Night's Dream*, 1.1.134), and the argument of this chapter is that that is indeed the theme of the sonnets. Love in the sonnets, far from being addressed only in its rose-tinted or romantic manifestations, is more often explicitly sexual, complicated, messy, and unsettling. Love in the sonnets is living, textured, never static, and contains more than a dash of rage, frustration, and even hate. Far fewer sonnets address love of the idealized variety that has made Sonnet 18 so popular than of sex, erotic transgression, and even "sexual deviance." For example, Sonnet 151 is devoted to the poet's penis in states of erection and post-coital detumescence, and in the course of the sonnets seminal emission (famously in Sonnet 129, "Th'expense of spirit [semen] in a waste of shame"), infidelity, adultery, homoeroticism, and venereal disease all make their appearance.

Before pursuing this line of inquiry, it is important to recall that there is considerable uncertainty about whether the events the poems describe correlate to Shakespeare's own life. Whether or not, then, such a parallel universe as "real life" exists for the sonnets, they intimate at least two other species of erotic transgression. First, the poet's desire for the youth, "my lovely boy" of Sonnet 126, who is at least old enough to father children, might be said to have pederastic overtones nonetheless because of the indications of the very substantial age difference between the aging poet and the much younger fair man. Secondly, whatever the early modern period meant by "black," whether brunette or negro, in the sonnets themselves black clearly means dark-complexioned and black-hearted: "Thy black is fairest in my judgment's place / In nothing art thou black save in thy deeds" (131.12–13). Here, the poet regards his mistress's dusky beauty as "fair," but he cannot put the same construction on her behavior. This troubled relationship is unquestionably a more transgressive alliance than the poet's relationship with the young man. While the poet excuses the young man's betrayal of him as a "sensual fault" (35.9), he reserves his anger and loathing for the "woman colored ill" (144.4). It is his love–hate relationship with her, and not his love for the worthy young man, that is colored (literally) by sexual perversity (de Grazia, 105). In this sense, Shakespeare extrapolates the conventional Petrarchan idea of the woman as an enemy because she is cruel and perhaps even sadistically enjoys the excruciating torment the poet-lover suffers as a result of her disdain. However, Laura, unlike the dark lady, was also the object of Petrarch's idolatrous worship. Thus in the sonnets two key aspects of Petrarchanism are divided along gender lines, so that the man becomes the object of Shakespeare's idolatrous admiration, idol worship (a sin he tries to excuse himself of in Sonnet 105, "Let not my love be called idolatry"), while the woman becomes his dangerous adversary.

Whereas in the lyric tradition of unconsummated Petrarchan love the poet-lover's misery arises from the fact that his mistress remains aloof, in Shakespeare's sonnets, in relation to the female addressee at least, the misery takes a more tangible form, namely the burning discomfort of venereal disease, a topic with which the sonnets toward the end of the Quarto are preoccupied. The poet's body betrays him in these poems. Wishing to be released from the bondage of love to his mistress, his physical cravings prevent his emancipation from her. The emphasis on erotic transgressions that the sonnets contain bespeaks much more the influence of Ovid than of Petrarch. In the *Ars Amatoria, The Art of Love*, the urbane Roman poet is largely concerned with (often adulterous) sex and how to find it, while Ovid's love elegies, the *Amores*, emphasize not as with Petrarch the impossibility of consummation, but rather the vagaries of actively sexual relationships.

True Love?

After the first seventeen sonnets urging the young man to marry and reproduce, there emerges a more complex and opaque narrative outline. The young man betrays the poet, with the "woman colored ill," and on her the poet unleashes a singularly visceral and specifically sexual disgust. The articulations of love for the young man are not, as in the case of the woman, polluted by contradictory feelings of revulsion. In these poems the poet seeks to express "The perfect ceremony of love's rite" (23.6), that is, the formula or convention of love's expression. Though the poet is tormented by suspicion, jealousy, and anxiety throughout, the nearest expressions of a complete purity of love occur, as we have noted, in relation to the young man section of the Quarto.

In 116, if we approach the sonnet in terms of an unfolding narrative, the poet seems to be separated from his beloved. Strangely impersonal in its tenor, this sonnet constitutes a proposition about the nature of love rather than a declaration of love to another person. Although it is thus embedded within the complex homoerotics of the sonnets, because it does not specify the gender of the addressee this sonnet is nonetheless a favorite reading at weddings. That the word "marriage" is in the very first line makes this a pertinent choice:

> Let me not to the marriage of true minds
> Admit impediments, love is not love

Which alters when it alteration finds,
Or bends with the remover to remove.
O no, it is an ever-fixed mark
That looks on tempests and is never shaken;
It is the star to every wand'ring bark,
Whose worth's unknown, although his height be taken.
Love's not Time's fool, though rosy lips and cheeks
Within his bending sickle's compass come,
Love alters not with his brief hours and weeks,
But bears it out even to the edge of doom:
   If this be error and upon me proved,
   I never writ, nor no man ever loved.

                (Sonnet 116)

Before we examine the many ways in which critics and editors have argued that this poem does *not* mean what it says, let us first take the poem at face value. Briefly, its argument is this: love is unchanging and unending, and anything that is otherwise is not love at all. If this can be proved false, then the poet will (in literary terms) eat his hat. Thus immutable and unconditional, love does not depend on its being returned in kind, that is, it does not "bend with the remover to remove." Likened to the pole star used for navigation, love is "the star to every wand'ring bark" (line 7). In its lyrical context, this image also alludes to one of Petrarch's most famous sonnets where the poet-lover is tossed on a stormy ocean, and unable to see the stars, which are Laura's eyes: "I despair of ever reaching port" ("*Passa la nave mia colma d'oblio*" ["My ship full of forgetful cargo sails"], Canzone 189). Shakespeare would have known a translation of Petrarch's sonnet first hand from a famous anthology of poetry known as *Tottel's Miscellany* (1557), which contained Sir Thomas Wyatt's translation of Petrarch's sonnet, "My galley charged with forgetfulness." Instead of Wyatt's Petrarchan despair, however, the poet in Shakespeare's sonnet expresses a confident statement of his faith in love that evokes the popular idea, derived from medieval Catholicism, of the Blessed Virgin as *stella maris*, star of the sea. Unlike Laura, or even Sir Philip Sidney's cruel mistress, Stella, *stella maris* is literally a guide to mariners who are at sail on the ocean, and, metaphorically, to all souls who are in this sense "at sea" until they are united with God. In claiming unwavering constancy as the mark of true love, Sonnet 116 looks toward the Christian concept of *agape*, the kind of unconditional love that transcends *eros* because it mirrors unconditional and immutable divine love. Run-of-the-mill human love, in contrast, is invariably flawed and all too enmeshed in the aesthetic appreciation of and carnal appetite for good looks, those "rosy lips and cheeks" that the poet knows will fade over time.

Generations of readers have understood this poem to constitute a lyrical definition of true love, that is, love that transcends time and is unperturbed by age and change. In contrast to this understanding, recent editors have argued that, far from articulating an ideal of love, this sonnet is an outright refutation of it. In one of the most forceful assertions of this line of argument, John Kerrigan writes: "This sonnet has been misread so often and so mawkishly that it is necessary to say at once, if brutally, that Shakespeare is writing about what cannot be attained" (Kerrigan, 53). It is fascinating that one of Shakespeare's most popular and often recited sonnets is the one critics feel does not lend itself to the kind of interpretive latitude typically associated with the sonnets and whose editions expound and extrapolate multiple valences of meaning and ambiguities of sense. Stephen Booth, though he accepts the sentiments of the poem at face value in a fashion that Kerrigan does not, is similarly suspicious not only of the poem's popularity, but also of his own response to it as a reader:

> Sonnet 116 is the most universally admired of Shakespeare's sonnets. Its virtues, however, are more than usually susceptible to dehydration in critical comment. The more one thinks about this grand, noble, absolute, convincing and moving gesture, the less there seems to be to it. One could demonstrate that it is just so much bombast, but having done so, one would have only to reread the poem to be again moved by it and convinced of its greatness. (Booth, 1977, 387)

Once he has his critic's hat on, Booth cannot enjoy the poem at all. The fact that critics and editors find this sonnet so emotionally and intellectually difficult is instructive: true love is a very touchy subject. Helen Vendler, in the same vein, regards the poem as a refutation of the argument for true love:

> My interpretation . . . suggest[s] that the usual interpretation is untrue, and not simply incomplete . . . Also, there are too many *no's* and *nor's*, *never's* and *not's* in this poem – one *nor*, two *no's*, two *never's*, and four *not's* – for it to seem a serene one. The prevalence of negations suggests

that this poem is not a definition, but rather a rebuttal – and all rebuttals encapsulate the argument they refute. (Vendler, 488)

Vendler reads the poem not as a definition but as a refutation of an argument about love staged almost as a rhetorical exercise to which we are not privy but which is implied by the poet's reasoning, and especially its insistent use of negatives – "never," "nor," "no." Vendler ingeniously emphasizes the poem's dramatic qualities as a speech in the course of a rather complicated legal debate.

Taken in their cultural context, however, the negatives may work to reinforce rather than undermine the straightforward proposition of the sonnet that true love is characterized by integrity and duration. For love, in its ideal and indeed divine manifestations, can be accessed only by reference to what it is not – *not* times's fool, etc. In fact, this is a standard mode of biblical discourse where it serves to express what is too great to be made apprehensible in either language or through images. Thus for St. John: "He that loveth not knoweth not God; for God is love" (1 John 4:8). Clearly, the evangelist means that God is love rather than the opposite. Proceeding by negatives in this way, the logic and reasoning of the sonnet, although they are complex, follow the same rhetorical strategy St. Paul uses to describe love, in a passage which, like Sonnet 116 itself, is also a standard reading at weddings:

> Though I speak with the tongues of men and Angels, and have not love, I am as sounding brass, or a tinkling cymbal. And though I had the gift of prophecy, and knew all secrets and all knowledge, yea, if I had all faith, so that I could remove mountaines and had not love, I were nothing. And though I feed the poor with all my goods, and though I give my body, that I be burned, and have not love, it profiteth me nothing . . . it is bountiful: love envieth not: love doth not boast it self: it is not puffed up: It doeth no uncomely thing: it seeketh not her own things: it is not provoked to anger: it thinketh not evil: It rejoyceth not in iniquity . . . (1 Corinthians 13:1–7, Geneva Bible [1587])

We cannot say what love is, only what it is not – prideful, envious, boastful, angry, selfish, and so on – but love is also possessed of a quality of permanence that will see out the demise not just of the sacred language of prophecy, but of language itself. Language, knowledge, will pass away and disappear, but this love will never cease. Paul's connection between love and prophetic discourse is significant in that predictive powers are often ascribed to poetry. In precisely the same rhetorical strategy of positive proposition via a series of negatives, Ovid prophesies that his verse will endure forever at the end of the *Metamorphoses*:

> Now have I brought a work to end which neither Jove's fierce wrath,
> **Nor** sword, **nor** fyre, **nor** freating age with all the force it hath
> Are able to abolish quite. . . . And all the world shall never
> Be able for to quench my name. For look how far so ever
> The Roman Empire by the right of conquest shall extend,
> So far shall all folk read this work. And time without all end
> (If Poets as by prophesy about the truth may aim)
> My life shall everlastingly be lengthened still by fame.
>
> (1.984–95, my emphasis)

Ovid's confident (and, as it turns out, accurate) divination of the future fate of his poetry in this passage is echoed very directly in Sonnet 55, "Not marble, nor the gilded monuments / Of princes shall out-live this powerful rhyme," a poem which also progresses by repetitions of the word "nor." In "the ending doom" of line 13, Sonnet 55 also echoes Sonnet 116's "edge of doom" as an expression of that which will perpetually endure.

Even if we acknowledge, as I think we must, the complexity, the philosophical and conceptual density around the expression of love in "Let me not to the marriage of true minds," it is still hard to accept that the consensus of generations of readers is so completely wide of the mark as some recent editors suggest. The English composer, Henry Lawes, adapted and expanded the lyric in the mid-seventeenth century. Since every adaptation is a reading and an interpretation of the original, Lawes offers a demonstration close to Shakespeare's lifetime that the poem was understood to mean what it says, namely that true love as opposed to its counterfeit does indeed withstand the test of time:

> Selfe blinding error seizeth all those minds;
> Who with false appellations call that love
> Which alters when it alteration finds
> Or with the mover hath a power to move
> Not much unlike the heretic's pretense
> That cites true scriptures but prevents their sense
>
> (Quoted Duncan-Jones, 1997, 465)

(Lawes's accusation of heresy might also be leveled at some of 116's commentators, not to mention at the lovers he describes.) Simplifying Shakespeare's sonnet even as he extrapolates it, Lawes forges a connection between religious belief and love that connects the lover with the Petrarchan tradition wherein he is a martyr consumed in its flames. This connection is explicit in Lawes's next stanza about the lover as a "flaming martyr in his holy ashes," and refers the listener to an erotic love so extreme that it approaches the divine.

The language Shakespeare uses to confute the idea that love fades with youth and beauty would have resonated for early modern readers with both biblical discourse and legal argument. The poem's admission of "impediments" echoes the marriage ceremony from the Book of Common Prayer, that is, the legally prescribed Church of England prayer book: "I require and charge you (as you will answer at the dreadful day of judgment, when the secrets of all hearts shall be disclosed) that if either of you know any impediment, why ye may not lawfully be joined in matrimony, that ye confess it." "The dreadful day of judgment" is also referred to as "Doomsday," echoed in line 12 in "the edge of doom." In a world where religious prescriptions were enforced not simply by a sense of private moral and ethical obligation but by the well-developed and active institutional apparatus of canon law and consistory (bishops') courts, the legally binding language of the marriage ceremony and its request for a declaration of lawful impediments is echoed in the language of the poem's last line, "writ" and "proved."

The close proximity of "error," "writ," and "doom" bespeaks a precise legal context. In fact, one of the most common forms of writ in early modern England was the "writ of error," while a "doom," as in the expression "the dooms of law," might refer to a range of terms, including law, a statute, enactment, ordinance, or decree, or to a formally pronounced judgment, or act of sentencing. Shakespeare used doom in the sense of a legal "term" (Hilary, Trinity, Michaelmas, Easter terms were the equivalents of our Fall, Spring, Summer semesters) that is of a fixed period of time in Sonnet 14, "Thy end is truth's and beauty's doom and date." In Macbeth 4.1.117, the sense is of the end of time: "What will the line stretch out to "th' crack of Doom?" Further, a "writ of error" was an important document in the legal system prior to the advent of the modern notion of appeal. The writ of error was forwarded to a higher court, usually to correct an inaccuracy of fact in the legal proceedings themselves. A writ of error referred would be brought in order to review and correct an error in the law committed in the process of legal proceedings and especially seeks to remedy a disparity between a legal judgment delivered by the court and the law itself. The discovery of such an error would result in a motion for a new trial. Early modern England was relentlessly litigious. Shakespeare himself not only had associations with the Inns of Court, such as Gray's Inn where, as we noted earlier, *The Comedy of Errors* (a play which is also interested in the definition of error) was first performed and where his patron the Earl of Southampton studied law, but had himself been involved in numerous lawsuits and legal proceedings. So what now seems like an obscure technicality would have been then well known to everyone whose social status was that of a gentleman or higher.

The final couplet, "If this be error and upon me proved / I never writ, nor no man ever loved," opens the way for a writ of error, that is, for a judicial review of decisions, whereby the record of proceedings in a given case would be sent to a superior court, "the court of error," for inspection. Crucially, from the legal point of view, and in this case a literary one, the only types of error that could be corrected were ones on the face of the record, that is, the correction of names, locations, and the like on the legal document, rather than the underlying facts of the case or points of law. The negatives of the final line, "never" and "no," combined with "ever" make disproof of the case impossible. From a legal perspective, it is impossible to prove that something has never, ever happened or never, ever existed.

Shakespeare is using a legal formula to demonstrate the depth of his love and commitment, and in fact the sonnet replicates legal reasoning in that the basis of all "proceedings in error," as they were known, was the record or "plea roll" containing the minutes of all stages in the legal action right down to the judgment. As J. H. Baker's *An Introduction to English Legal History* explains, "The record was invested with such a sacred finality that it was accepted as conclusive evidence of whatever it contained" (Baker, 118). Shakespeare is claiming precisely this kind of legal accuracy for his judgment upon love, namely that true love is eternal.

The language of "error" and the business of legal proceedings reassert themselves in the very next sonnet, 117, which shifts from constant love to the more volatile exchanges between the poet and the young man. Despite his almost feudal obligations to attend upon the young man, the poet has neglected him for other, less worthy companions. The language of this sonnet again insists, but with more of a sense of legal metaphor than the specific legality of 116, that the beloved should "Book both my willfulness and errors down" (117.9). The poet is willing to be charged with misconduct by the young man, but urges him to defer punishment:

> Since my appeal says I did strive to prove
> The constancy and virtue of your love.
>
> (117.13–14)

Admitting that his absence from the youth has been willful, that he has not merely drifted apart from the young man but has abetted the action of outside influences, the poem evokes the Latin derivation of the word *errare*, to wander or to stray:

> That I have hoisted sail to all the winds
> Which should transport me farthest from your sight.
>
> (117.7–8)

The poet has "strayed" in the sexual sense, and the language here echoes the wandering bark of 116, and the "saucy bark" in the ocean of the young man's love in Sonnet 80. "Sail" suggests ample and billowing skirts, as in the ironic joke on petticoat-chasing in relation to the Nurse in *Romeo and Juliet*: "A sail, a sail!" (2.3.89–90).

Critics have tended to see the poems that preceded the great Sonnet 116 as qualifying its argument for constancy. However, there is a sense in which 117 proves that the young man continued to love the poet, even though the latter aroused his jealousy by absence and neglect.

Lovesickness

For all their glimpses of the magnificent possibilities of love, the young man sonnets are not without their sense that even when the poet's affections are addressed to the most sublime of objects, love, or at least sexual desire, is by its very nature predisposed to bring about a physical and psychological disequilibrium in those who experience it. In

Sonnet 118, the poet has willfully made himself sick by mixing with bad company, which he likens to taking an emetic: "As to prevent our maladies unseen, / We sicken [make ourselves sick] to shun sickness when we purge." The sonnet suggests also that the poet has become sated with the youth's good qualities, and has roamed partly for the sake of variety, but also to prevent even worse infidelities:

> Even so being full of your ne'er-cloying sweetness,
> To bitter sauces did I frame my feeding;
> And sick of welfare found a kind of meetness,
> To be diseased ere that there was true needing.
> Thus policy in love t' anticipate
> The ills that were not, grew to faults assured,
> And brought to medicine a healthful state
> Which rank of goodness would by ill be cured.
>   But thence I learn and find the lesson true,
>   Drugs poison him that so fell sick of you.

All love, even love for the young man, is a sickness, but this is an indisposition incapable of cure; rather, an attempt to remedy this disease would be poisonous. While the sonnet ends on a positive note in terms of the poet's rededication of his love to the young man, it contains nonetheless a sense that when love does go smoothly, palatably, it compels the poet to seek elsewhere: sweetness and vomit are too close to one another in this poem for lyrical comfort. Drawing upon dietary practices of the time and health regimens that included purgatives and laxatives, Sonnet 118 conveys the intimate and unsavory reality of the poet's body – vomiting, defecating, and beset with addictive behaviors. For all that, these are relatively benign illnesses – common maladies with everyday, albeit unpleasant, cures.

We enter the realms of fatal and venereal disease in the dark lady sonnets. In Sonnet 144, the poet's two loves are now sexually intimate with one another, or at least so the poet suspects. The youth here figures as the celestial spirit and the woman as hell's angel, the dark abyss of the poet's psychosexual and indeed lyrical energy. The verbal and thematic focal point of the poem is "hell," a reference to the allegedly infernal reaches of the woman's vagina, stemming from the Old English etymology of "hell," *helan*, meaning "to hide" and, by extension, anything dark and out of sight. Published in a slightly different form in *The Passionate Pilgrim* (1599), the original spelling and punctuation there, with repeated rhymes of words ending in "ll," serves to emphasize this point:

> For being both to me: both, to each friend
> I guess one Ang**ell** in anothers h**ell**:
> The truth I sh**all** not know, but live in doubt,
> T**ill** my bad Ang**ell** fire my good one out.
> (*Passionate Pilgrim*, sig A4)

This sonnet describes an infernally jealous vision of the angels *in flagrante delicto*: the male angel is "in" the vagina of the female one.

Indebted to the medieval dramatic tradition of the psychomachia and Everyman, whose soul is fought over by the spiritual agents of both heaven and hell, the "fire" of the last line is moral corruption and specifically venereal disease. Shakespeare's great rival, Marlowe, had staged an early modern version of this medieval tradition where good and evil spirits sought to win the soul of Dr. Faustus, and Shakespeare himself penned another version of the story in *Othello* where a woman who has a demon in her name, "the divine Des**demon**a," is played off against the demonic Iago who compels Othello to "curse his better angel from his side" (5.2.208). A less sinister rendition of the idea of diabolical femininity, a sort of early modern equivalent of "the devil in the blue dress," was to be found in the first book of Sidney's *Arcadia* and John Weever's *Faunus and Melliflora* (1600). Although more benign than Shakespeare's sonnet, the ferocious struggle against vainly repressed sexual temptation is similarly although humorously figured as a precipitous headlong dive into perdition: "For many one for Hell, not Heaven would pray, / If such she devil were in Hell to play."

There is nothing nearly so light-hearted as Weever's jest in the tenor of the sonnets addressed to the woman colored ill, pervaded as they are by images of death and disease. Shakespeare thus takes the conventional notion that love is an insanity inducing malady, with which he is now "frantic-mad" (147.10), and extrapolates it into the far more troubling notion that, as he puts it in 147, "Desire is death" (line 8). Further, in its final couplet, this sonnet expresses the idea that in being betrayed by the woman, the poet has a sudden change of perspective upon her:

> For I have sworn thee fair, and thought thee bright,
> Who art as black as hell, as dark as night.

Betrayal is not, alas, unique in the annals of human experience, but the sonnets' treatment of it finds a vivid literary precursor in Ovid's poetry. In the *Amores* Book 3, Ovid discovers his beloved Corinna's infidelity after she has given him the slip by feigning sickness:

> Why remind you of all your sordid lies, those broken
>   Promises, worthless oaths
> You swore to my undoing, the young men who gave you private
>   Signals at parties, coded exchanges? "She's sick,"
> They told me: at once I hurried back like a madman, found you
> The picture of health – and in my rival's arms.
>
>   (*Amores*, 3.11A.21–6)

The translation above is a modern one, but this verse might have been particularly present in Shakespeare's consciousness since it was one of Ovid's elegies translated as follows by Christopher Marlowe:

> Long have I borne much, mad thy faults me make:
>   Dishonest love, my wearied breast forsake! . . .
>   My love was cause that more mens love she seized.
> What should I tell her vain tongue's filthy lies.
> And, to my loss, god-wronging perjures?
> What secret becks in banquets with her youths.
> With privy signs, and talk dissembling truths?
> Hearing her to be sick, I thither ran,
> But with my rival sick she was not then.
>
>   (*Elegia* X.1–2, 20–7, Burnett ed., 65)

Ovid's success as a poet has, he tells us, lured other men toward his mistress in a way that resembles the fact that in Shakespeare's Sonnet 144, the mutual attraction of the angels is anchored in the poet. Like the poet in the sonnets, too, Ovid has a love–hate relationship with his mistress:

> A fugitive from your vices, I'm lured back by your beauty:
>   Your morals turn me off, your body on.
> So I can live neither with you nor without you, I don't seem
>   To know my own mind.
>
>   (*Amores*, 3.11B.5–8)

Or, as Marlowe's translation puts it:

> I'll hate, if I can, if not, love 'gainst my will . . .
> I fly her lust, but follow beauty's creature;
> I loathe her manners, love her body's feature.
> Nor with thee, nor without thee can I live
> (Elegia X.35–9, Burnett ed., 65–6)

Both Ovid's *Amores* and the sonnets convey the underside of love. That this dimension of erotic experience (literally the dark side in the sonnets) is associated with the feminine is in part the result of the cultural impetus to deny and repress femininity and sexuality in many facets of early modern culture. The more the poet is locked in struggle to push the feminine and everything associated with it out of awareness, the more the desire for the woman returns in increasingly fearful, unwanted manifestations.

The self-induced malady the poet experienced with the young man is a considerable distance from the galloping venereal disease the poet contracted from his female lover. The very last poems of the sequence discover the poet in what was known as a "sweating tub," a bath of almost boiling water, "a seething bath" (153.7) thought to alleviate symptoms of syphilis and gonorrhea: "a bath and healthful remedy" (154.11). The last two sonnets, the Quarto's *envoy* (literally, its send-off), lead us not to the higher realms of human feeling but to the gross, physical effects that result when love (or at least sexual consummation) is literally rather than metaphorically a sickness. The poet plays with the contrast between the literary language of love and the medical facts of disease in 153 and 154. Both sonnets begin with the image of Cupid, leading the reader to expect a sonnet rather more "sugared" (to use Frances Meres's description of the sonnets to which he had been privy prior to their publication) than the acidic aftertaste these sonnets leave for the entire collection.

In 153, while Cupid is asleep, a handmaid of the goddess of chastity, Diana the huntress, steals his arrow and quenches it in a cold mountain fountain. The effect is to heat the water and create a healing pool, where people take restorative baths. Up to this point in the story the poem tells, we are in the realms of conventional, classical mythic imagery. (Indeed, both 153 and 154 take up a conceit from Greek poetry, which was handed down to the Renaissance in a six-line Greek epigram by a fifth-century Byzantine poet, Marianus Scholasticus, from whence it was translated into Latin and other European languages.) At line 9, however, the shadow of the Petrarchan volta or turn, Shakespeare makes his own addendum to the tale. Cupid's torch takes light at "my mistress' eye" (153.9) and, being a naughty little boy, the god of love wants to try out the power of his renovated ammunition, and does so on the poet. Now, sick with love, the poet must resort to the magically heated waters, but these are of no avail because the cure lies, like the disease, in the eyes of the poet's mistress.

The sense that medicine and disease are not strictly distinct is an idea Shakespeare has pursued (as we saw earlier in Sonnet 118, where drugs can poison even a sick man) throughout the sonnets:

> Cupid laid by his brand and fell asleep,
> A maid of Dian's this advantage found,
> And his love-kindling fire did quickly steep
> In a cold valley-fountain of that ground:
> Which borrowed from this holy fire of Love,
> A dateless lively heat still to endure,
> And grew a seething bath which yet men prove,
> Against strange maladies a sovereign cure:
> But at my mistress' eye Love's brand new-fired,
> The boy for trial needs would touch my breast,
> I sick withal the help of bath desired,
> And thither hied a sad distempered guest.
>   But found no cure, the bath for my help lies,
>   Where Cupid got new fire; my mistress' eyes.

Although the poet has assured his readers in 130 that his mistress's eyes are "nothing like the sun," they have here a prodigious power to ignite even the dampest of Cupid's suggestively phallic brands. However, given the numerous associations in these poems of the woman with hell, the fire is likely to be that of an infernal conflagration. Shakespeare reiterates this story in the volume's final sonnet, and the result for the poet's love-induced ailment is the same: there is no cure. Both of these poems tell the story of love from two perspectives, that of the diminutive god of love, Cupid, and from the point of view of the poet-lover. However, in the final poem, while the poet has the last word, he enters the poem (as, for that matter, does his mistress) very belatedly, at line 12:

> . . . I by my mistress' thrall,
> Came there for cure and this by that I prove,
> Love's fire heats water, water cools not love.
> (Sonnet 154.12–14)

The poet's drama of love is itself immersed in a very ancient narrative and a well-worn set of dynamics: Eros, virgin nymphs, fountains, passion, heat. For all that, the poet insists on the extremity of his disease, and we leave him at the end of the sonnets in the rather undignified posture of a sick man in a sweating tub. This is not a gloriously poetic ending. Even the biblical reference here to the *Song of Solomon* does not dispatch the venereal resonances:

> O set me as a seal upon thine heart, and as a seal upon thine arm: for love is mighty as the death, and jealousy as the hell. Her coals are coals of fire, and a very vehement flame [of the Lord]: so that many waters are not able to quench love, neither may the streams drown it . . . (8.6–7, Bishop's Bible [1568])

While at first this biblical passage may seem at odds with the proposition of the sonnet, its argument is in fact surprisingly consistent with it. The sense of the passage is that absolutely nothing, neither death nor jealousy nor flood, can destroy pure love. To this catalog of afflictions Shakespeare adds venereal disease.

CHAPTER 5

Numbers

"Reckoning time" (115.5) is presented in the sonnets as a kind of depraved accountant who is the enemy of love and life. As the destroyer of youth and beauty, we might reasonably expect time to be the direct antithesis of the poet. Yet, he is not, for no matter how much ire the poet directs at time, on closer inspection the two are to be found engaging in precisely the same, rather than reverse, activities.[1] Certainly, in the early sonnets, the poet himself rather than a personification of time brandishes time's scythe over the head of the young man as he issues his threats about the immediate necessity of reproduction. The poet admonishes the youth about time in an attempt to save him from it, but there are moments when it seems that if time could talk, he would sound exactly like the poet: "thou . . . diest, unless thou get a son" (7.13–14). This sense of collusion between time and the poet, or perhaps more accurately, these moments of complicity with time's decrees are significant in that one of the poet's principal occupations is precisely that of "reckoning" or counting time. The idea that such calculation was the vital medium for poetic expression is reflected in the early modern use of "numbers" as a synonym for verse. In *Romeo and Juliet*, Mercutio teases Romeo that one of the results of falling in love will be love poetry, and the specific form of that poetry will be the Petrarchan sonnet: "Now is he for the *numbers* that Petrarch flowed in" (2.4.38–9).[2]

The argument of this chapter, then, is that the sonnets demonstrate a thematic preoccupation with numbers of various kinds precisely because counting constitutes one of the essential elements of poetry. The poet's first task is to count out the metrical beat of the sonnet.

Time in poetry, just as much as on the clock face, is fundamentally *about* counting. Sonnet 12, for instance, "When I do count the clock that tells the time," marks out the iambic beat like a metronome. Of course the predictability of the meter here is designed to reflect the progress of time on the clock face, which renders temporal progression as counting. In Sonnet 106, a poem about "wasted" time, which is to say, *past* time, the poet ponders poetic tradition, "making beautiful old rhyme" (106.3). Rhyme refers of course to fundamental features of poetry and of the sonnet tradition in particular. This patterning of similar sounds is such an intrinsic aspect of versification that "rhyme" is often used as a synonym for poetry, as in "my rhyme" (17.14), "barren rhyme" (16.4), and in reference to the rival poets, "their rhyme" (32.7), "rhymers" (38.10), "powerful rhyme" (55.2), "beautiful old rhyme" (106.3), "poor rhyme" (107.11). The poet, then, must "reckon" the iambic line, number his fourteen lines, and keep to his largely unvarying sonnet rhyme scheme ABAB CDCD EFEF GG. Crucially, in terms of rhyme and meter, Shakespeare follows literary precedent and eschews innovation and variation, adhering, without much in the way of deviation, to the sonnet form of the 1590s. In this sense, Shakespeare's sonnets are captured in time, their metrical art being very little different from that of Sir Philip Sidney's *Astrophil and Stella*, published in 1591 (Wright, 76). Thus Shakespeare's lyrical numbers are just as predictable, relentless, and unwavering as those of his antagonist, time.

Number One

In Sonnet 20, beginning "A woman's face with nature's own hand painted, / Hast thou the master mistress of my passion," the line that has aroused astonishing interpretive furor about whether this expresses the poet's homosexual desire for the youth, is the one in which the poet plays on the fundamental distinction between *something*, that is, male genitalia, *and nothing*, female genitalia, quibbling that nature has equipped the beloved with "**one** thing to my purpose nothing":

> A woman's face with nature's own hand painted,
> Hast thou the master mistress of my passion,

A woman's gentle heart but not acquainted
With shifting change as is false women's fashion,
An eye more bright than theirs, less false in rolling:
Gilding the object whereupon it gazeth,
A man in hue all hues in his controlling,
Which steals men's eyes and women's souls amazeth.
And for a woman wert thou first created,
Till nature as she wrought thee fell a-doting,
And by addition me of thee defeated,
By adding one thing to my purpose nothing.
    But since she pricked thee out for women's pleasure,
    Mine be thy love and thy love's use their treasure.

Typically, this sonnet is addressed in terms of the matter of sexual identity, as we saw in chapter 2, by those who wish to claim that Shakespeare was heterosexual using the infamously slippery line 12, "By adding one thing to my purpose nothing," as evidence that the poet was indifferent to the youth's "thing." Those wishing to prosecute the contrary argument have claimed (more plausibly, given the context of the young man sonnets) that the youth's thing is not an impediment to the poet's desire, but only to the possibility of a reproductive sexual relationship with the young man. In addition, a host of critical fence sitters argue that the poem is simply ambivalent, and that readers are not intended to take this sonnet as a definitive statement about the poet's sexual preferences. That, at any rate, is the range of interpretive opinion on "one thing to my purpose nothing." However, if we broaden the interpretive literary context of this line, the marked similarity with a line from Shakespeare's greatest rival Christopher Marlowe's *Hero and Leander* reveals what may have been a mutual influence, since we do not know whether Marlowe wrote his epyllion before Shakespeare wrote Sonnet 20, or vice versa. In *Hero and Leander*, a sexually uninformed but amorous youth, Leander, attempts to dissuade the beautiful maiden, Hero, from keeping her vow of chastity with the argument that "One is no number." *Number* in early modern English meant "more than one" as opposed to our modern singular locution, *a number*, or a single digit. The line playfully suggests a truth about the number one, but also that relationships are in essence about becoming more than one thing, more than oneself.

In Sonnet 136, the similarity to Marlowe's "one is no number" is again striking:

Among a number one is reckoned none.
Then in the number let me pass untold,
Though in thy store's account I one must be,
For nothing hold me, so it please thee hold
That nothing me a something sweet to thee.

(136.8–11)

In 136 the poet begs not to be counted, "to pass untold," by the woman who is now positioned as someone who inventories her lovers. The implication here is one of a clandestine relationship: "untold" because of not telling anybody. Yet, there is also a sense of being only one and therefore quantitatively insufficient to register. Conversely, the idea of being "untold" conveys the sense of having transcended all means of enumeration. The modern equivalent of this latter sense is something like the word "priceless," meaning so valuable, so beyond any scale of valuation, that a price cannot be put on it, as well as something that, because by its very nature cannot be put on the market for sale, is in a sense also "worthless." Value thus comes full circle and so the worthless and the priceless converge. The poet bids the woman to suspend her calculations in relation to him and "thy store's account," though it is also a pun on "a cunt" because "count" and "cunt" were homonymic in early modern English. This is particularly important because the sonnet suggests the activity of a businesswoman, and in this instance particularly the "business" of prostitution. However, it is also possible that the woman is one of the frugal housewives presented in numerous conduct books of the period. In their most idealized form, such women were chaste, obedient, and industrious wives whose role as "helpmeet" to their husbands often involved active participation and involvement in their husbands' business affairs. However, in *Othello*, Emilia is a careful housewife who would nonetheless consider adultery if it offered sufficient material advantages. The women of the immensely popular genre of city comedies offer similar portraits of canny married women who are very much involved in the world of merchandising and exchange.

Since 136 is one of the "Will" sonnets, much has been made of the ribald misogyny of the poem, some critics dismissing it as merely a verbal game not to be taken seriously, while others see it as grounds for indictment of the poet's attitudes toward women. The tone of this poem *is* complicated, and shifting. There is something especially poignant, as well as potentially obscene given the context, about the poet enjoining the woman to "hold me" as "something sweet to thee." Troubled by the woman's promiscuity, the poet is even more disturbed by the application of her financial acumen to the complexities of sexual exchange. However, the reader is also almost compelled to engage in computation and count the uses of the word "will" and the words that rhyme with it:

> Will will fulfill the treasures of thy love,
> Ay, fill it full with wills, and my will one;
> (136.5–6)

The "will one" may mean either that the poet's "will," his penis, is one among many admitted to the dark lady's orifice, or that his member is uniquely able to satisfy her. This idea requires no fewer than six expressions of "will" comprised of four uses of the word and two rhyme words, namely "fill" and "fulfill." Even, then, as the poet enjoins the woman not to count him among her lovers, he begs to be received to the exclusion of all others, as *the* "one." He cannot desist from the counting, rhyming, and repeating that are the intrinsically poetic elements of the sonnet, and which mirror his anxiety about all the multitude of "wills" he fears his lover entertains.

To return to the young man sonnets where issues of number manifest rather differently, in Sonnet 122, in a line that refers to an antiquated method of accounting, the poet assures the youth that his love transcends the necessity for calculation: "Nor need I tallies thy dear love to score" (line 10). A score was itself a number, a quantity, twenty, the same as that of Shakespeare's most sexually ambivalent sonnet. However, the predominant reference here, though unfamiliar to modern readers, would have been well known in Shakespeare's time as a rather primitive system of keeping accounts pervasive throughout the medieval era and prior to the advent of widespread literacy. The "score and tally" was a system of marking sticks with notches in order to keep a record of financial transactions such as wages, hours of labor, debts, or of quantities of goods. Crucially, the scored stick was split lengthwise so that both parties to a given transaction could keep track of it. At the end of a given exchange, tally sticks would be aligned again and the transaction completed.[3] Even though in early modern

England both the method and material of accounting largely had changed from scores on wood to mathematical computation on paper, the "score and tally" persisted as a popular method of accounting among the uneducated.[4]

> Thy gift, thy tables, are within my brain
> Full charactered with lasting memory,
> Which shall above that idle rank remain
> Beyond all date even to eternity.
> Or at the least, so long as brain and heart
> Have faculty by nature to subsist,
> Till each to razed oblivion yield his part
> Of thee, thy record never can be missed:
> That poor retention could not so much hold,
> Nor need I tallies thy dear love to score,
> Therefore to give them from me was I bold,
> To trust those tables that receive thee more:
> > To keep an adjunct to remember thee
> > Were to import forgetfulness in me.

On the face of it, 122 is a poem in which the poet seeks to justify the fact that he has given away a book, which has been written in by the young man, and to reassure him of his fidelity, the poet declares that he needs no external reminders because the youth is always in his heart and mind. The book the poet has given away is probably a commonplace book, the "waste blanks" (line 10) or blank pages of the journal the poet gave to him in Sonnet 77. The poet claims he gave the book away because his mind and heart serve as more reliable and durable repositories of the young man than any written record, which can all too easily be destroyed, deleted, or erased. The poet then turns to the solid score and tally, materially more durable than paper. For all that he dismisses this system as a primitive, petty account keeping, throughout the young man sonnets the poet in fact keeps careful score of the smaller infidelities and great betrayals (as in Sonnets 34, 35, 40, 41, and 121, among others), and does so despite all protestations to the contrary. He keeps a specifically financial count in images, for instance in the problem of overvaluation in Sonnet 125 of those "pitiful thrivers" (line 8) who have lost everything by "paying too much rent" (125.6).

In "numbers number" (17.6), then, Shakespeare forges a specific connection between the practice of enumeration and the process of poetic composition. Sonnet 17 is famously concerned with the urgency of reproduction, with the business of making "another thee." Over and over again, the poet insists that the one life, the single life of the young man, and his one lifetime are insufficient. The poet is insistent that this life must be augmented and perpetuated both by his own art and by the young man's children.

> Who will believe my verse in time to come
> If it were filled with your most high deserts?
> Though yet heaven knows it is but as a tomb
> Which hides your life, and shows not half your parts:
> If I could write the beauty of your eyes,
> And in fresh numbers number all your graces,
> The age to come would say this poet lies,
> Such heavenly touches ne'er touched earthly faces.
> So should my papers (yellowed with their age)
> Be scorn'd, like old men of less truth than tongue,
> And your true rights be termed a poet's rage,
> And stretched meter of an antique song.
> > But were some child of yours alive that time,
> > You should live twice in it, and in my rhyme.

The opening interrogative of the poem suggests that the aim of poetry is plausibility in face of the dangers of hyperbole. The initial element of quantification here comes at the end of the first quatrain, where the sonnet is evaluated as having the power to represent "half" the reality of the young man because it obscures his merits even as it strives to portray them. The aspiration to achieve mimetic accuracy, "If I could write the beauty of your eyes," would require innovative powers of poetic technique, "in fresh numbers number all your graces." The effect of the adjacent and alliterative "numbers number" serves to replicate rather than augment the reader's image of the young man, but again emphasizes that both the content and the function of metrical counting is "numbers." However, even the achievement of this poetic ideal would not be believed because it would be taken for the "stretched meter of an antique song," that is, the systematic rhythm of an outdated and inept metrical composition. Strictly speaking then, the inadequacies of the old lyric are not those of exaggeration but of attenuated metrical lines. That is, such lines, from the point of view of poetic counting, simply do not add up. Biological reproduction is, however, superior in producing an adequate representation of the young man, allowing him to live "twice." In a sense, this is erroneous arithmetic: would the young man not in fact live *thrice* – in his own life, in his child, and in the poem? But the poet takes only the child and the poem into his calculations, discounting – perhaps on the grounds that "one is no number" – the original life from which these copies, biological and poetic, have been taken. This exemplifies a fundamental proposition of the young man sonnets, namely, that *one* is never enough.

Multiplication

Shakespeare's unorthodox arithmetic in the Quarto also includes a preponderance of financial imagery. Surprisingly, this often appears in sonnets whose main theme is something far more conventionally poetic, such as time and death. For example, in Sonnet 100, the poet asks the Muse to give him recompense figured in specifically financial terms for time lost: "Return forgetful Muse, and straight redeem, / In gentle numbers time so idly spent" (100.5–6). The "gentle numbers" are verses, but they are to be "redeemed," or cashed in with interest in the manner of a financial bond. In Sonnet 79, line 3, "gracious numbers" are now "decayed" because of loss of patronage to a rival poet. Sonnet 74 imagines dying as being taken to debtor's prison without any possibility of bail; Sonnet 75 treats a miser and his wealth; 109 ponders inheritance; Sonnet 30 addresses the matter of legal settlement; financial compensation also appears in Sonnet 30; auditing in Sonnets 49 and 126; poor financial management, "unthrift," in 9 and 13, and "waste" of both money and time in 1, 9, 12, 15, 30, 45, 77, 106, 125, and 129; stinginess, "niggarding," occurs in 1, 4, 72; mortgages are addressed in 134; interest (31); payments (30); value, "worth" (72); "engrossing" (133), or "making a famine where abundance lies" (1.7), a practice especially associated with grain hoarding to artificially inflate prices; and leases (such as 146.5, "so short a lease"), loans (6), rent (125), abundance, lack, and greed. Sometimes these images occur at startling moments. In Sonnet 142, for example, the poet's admission to sleeping with other men's wives is expressed as a crime against property, one of having "Robbed others' beds' revenues of their rents" (142.8).

If the above list is deliberately belabored it is because Shakespeare insistently reiterates these financial terms. Hitherto alien to the genre of love poetry, this language is also irredeemably shaped by the context of what the new economic developments brought about by the emerging system of capitalism that was rapidly supplanting feudal modes of economic organization and production in England at this time. Shakespeare, an entrepreneur himself, thus appropriated an aristocratic genre, the sonnet, to articulate social and erotic aspirations, often infused, especially in the first part of the sequence addressed to the young man, with the language of emerging mercantilism. The early sonnets present issues of biological, financial, and artistic production and reproduction in an erotic sphere defined by economic conditions that were coming to be dominated by time (the youth must *hurry up* and have children) and scarcity (the specter of impending dearth haunts the sonnets) rather than by organic and biological imperatives.

"Revenue," that is, the return on sexual and financial investment in the multiplication of people and wealth, is one of the controlling themes of the young man sonnets. From the very first line of the first sonnet in the 1609 Quarto, the poet insists on the duty to obey the biblical injunction to increase and multiply, not in a biblical context but in an economic and financial one: "From fairest creatures we desire increase" (1.1). Indeed, "breeding" in the period meant both making interest on an investment and the production of progeny, especially to ensure the lineage of inheritance.

In Sonnet 37, a sonnet which suggests the precarious financial and emotional dependence of the poet on his beloved patron, the poet tells the young man that "I in thy abundance am suffic'd" and that his good wishes for the youth make him "ten times happy me." The meaning of "increase" here is simultaneously financial and reproductive. There are also biblical echoes, especially of the New Testament parable of the talents, where in Matthew's gospel servants are entrusted the master's wealth in the expectation that they will increase it.

One of the most significant aspects of capitalist development was the practice of charging interest on loans, whose moral and social ramifications Shakespeare explored in some detail in *The Merchant of Venice*. Although usury was officially proscribed in medieval England, people found ways of circumventing legal restrictions on the practice. In England, before 1624 the legal limit on rates of interest was 10 percent.[5] This rate is reflected in Sonnet 6, when the poet tries to persuade the youth that in having a child he will not be profiting from illicit or exorbitant interest but engaging in a perfectly legitimate transaction. In the process, Shakespeare makes a distinction between "use," literally, the business of breeding human beings, and "usury," the proscribed breeding of money that constitutes illegitimate gain:

> That **use** is not forbidden **usury**,
> Which happies those that pay the willing loan;
> That's for thy self to breed another thee,
> Or ten times happier be it ten for one,
> Ten times thy self were happier than thou art,
> If ten of thine ten times refigured thee
>
> (Sonnet 6)

The repetitions here function as the lyrical reflection of the idea of interest – of getting more of what you started with – and ten is repeated five times, thus with 500 percent interest. The youth will be "refigured" in the sense of making miniature versions of himself, but also able to "figure" or calculate the worth of his life in the number of his progeny, especially since the gentry and aristocracy married for financial advantage.

Some of Shakespeare's contemporaries argued vehemently against usury. In 1591, Henry Smith wrote that:

> usury is a kind of cruelty, and a kind of extortion, and a kind of persecution, and therefore the want of love doth make Usurers: for if there were love there would bee no usury, no deceit, no extortion, no slandering, no revenging, no oppression, but wee should love in peace and joy and contentment like the Angels (quoted Herman, 272).

In the sonnets, unnatural reproduction, the *breeding* of money, the ostensibly iniquitous practice of usury, rather than being the antithesis of love was in fact structurally analogous to it. That is, the poet's love for the young man, the desire to have more of him, to have him multiplied to the power of ten, is arguably an instance of insatiable greed of precisely the kind Smith condemned. Yet Sonnet 6 picks up another strand of the contemporary economic argument in his claim that "use" is not usury. Another contemporary, Roger Fenton, also worked through this distinction:

> the usury of nature, that most innocent and primitive increase which the earth yieldeth in fruit unto man for his seed sown. . . . Neither are we to meddle with that supernatural usury which passeth between God and man: where sometimes man play[s the] usurer, and lending unto God by giving to the poor that he may receive an hundred fold. . . . Sometimes God himself is the usurer, lending talents unto men to lay out that he may receive in his own again, *with advantage*, as we translate it (quoted Herman, 272).

In Fenton's terms, "nature's usury," like Shakespeare's "use," is a model of organic, divinely organized increase perfectly analogous to usury rather than a sign of its contravention.[6]

In addition to the procreative connotations of the term in this sonnet, "use" had a specific and legally defined meaning in the period. "Uses" constituted the surviving remnants of the feudal financial system, and had been a key point in Henry VIII's relationship with the governing classes in Parliament in the 1530s. In the medieval era landowners could hold land from the crown in exchange for "knight service," to which they could be called upon by the king as a way of providing military support whenever it was needed. When such a landowner died, his heir was required to pay duty on the land in order to inherit it. The practice of "use" offered a way of circumventing these duties: the landowner ceded legal ownership of his property to a body of trustees, who administered it on his behalf, and, on his demise, on behalf of his heir. As Michael Graves points out, "The 'use' had an additional advantage: the trust never died and so, as most feudal dues were death duties, they were evaded" (Graves, 91). In an attempt to rectify the evasion of these payments, Henry forced through Parliament the Statute of Uses in 1536, which restored the monarch's feudal right to the fees, only to become one of the causes of the most significant challenge to Henry's power in the period, the Pilgrimage of Grace in 1536. The end result was a compromise enacted in the Statute of Wills (1540), whereby the crown was entitled to a third of these dues.

There is, then, a dense and legally informed strand of reasoning in Sonnet 6 that claims "use" as the legitimate financial right of the youth and his heirs, and also intimates a third party, the trust (the administrators) with whom the poet is structurally aligned. "Then not let winter's ragged hand deface" thus speaks to the necessity of having an heir for the transmission of land and property as much as it does to the requirement that beauty and youth survive in the world; or rather, youth and beauty in this sonnet are very much defined by the degree to which they are endowed with the advantage of property.

Even when he most idealizes the young man, the poet has financial matters on his mind: leases, rent, debt, payments feature continually in his lyrical musings. Thus, in 18, "Shall I compare thee to a summer's day," by the end of the first quatrain the poet has turned the duration of summer into a specifically financial term: "summer's *lease* hath all too short a date" (18.4); by the Shakespearean shadow of the Petrarchan "turn," at line 9, "Nor lose possession of that fair thou ow'st," he invokes the spectacle of eviction (as in to "lose possession" of a property) and debt, even as he counters it with the assertion that poetry will save the beautiful youth from this fate. This is not the language of someone who assumes that his financial substance is secure, but rather of someone who is literally counting every penny, or more accurately, counting absolutely everything that he encounters. Crucially, in 18 as elsewhere in the Quarto, time is money. Far from being simply a grand metaphysical abstraction, therefore, time becomes specifically financial time: the duration of a fixed term in which interest is accrued, or more often, the expiration of a term at which time a debt must be settled.

In a more embittered tone, Sonnet 87 cues what appears to be the end of the relationship with the poet, an ending initiated by the young man. The opening sestet is relentlessly financial:

> Farewell, thou art too dear for my possessing,
> And like enough thou know'st thy estimate,
> The charter of thy worth gives thee releasing:
> My bonds in thee are all determinate.
> For how do I hold thee but by thy granting,
> And for that riches where is my deserving?
>
> (Sonnet 87)

"[T]oo dear" implies not only too well cherished, but also too expensive and suggests the class difference between the aristocratic youth and the lowly poet. Similarly, "my possessing" elaborates on the more obvious implication of the emotional pleasures of intimacy with the sense of purchase and legal ownership, while "worth" and "estimate" again harp on the issue of financial appraisal. The poet's "bonds" are also social ties freighted with the notion of legal obligation, and even "hold" functions as a legal metaphor, as in "to hold title to" (Booth, 1977, 290). Now that the poet no longer has a legal claim on the young man's affections, he can receive only the "riches" (actual wealth) as well as the bounty of the young man's superior personal qualities: he must rely on the young man's inclination to generosity. However, even this kind of giving, a form of generosity that is free of the constraint of social or legal obligation, is conceived in terms of a "grant" or charter, "The charter of thy worth." The sonnet moves from a more mundane economic register of carefully specified legal entitlement in the lexicon of possession and bond to a model of sovereign largess – charters were the province of the crown. That "The charter of thy worth gives thee releasing" indicates that the young man's social privilege meant that he was never truly bound by the less exalted legal obligations he had been party to with the poet.

In the final couplet of this sonnet, the poet claims that he was dreaming that he was a king, entitled to the wealth of love that he had hitherto claimed from the young man. Shakespeare's Sonnet 87 in fact reverses the sentiments of Sir Philip Sidney's Sonnet 69 in *Astrophil and Stella*. Sidney's sonnet claims possession of Stella, whose superiority is figured in terms of the metaphor of a feudal relationship between the all-powerful woman who is placed on a lofty pedestal and the man who sues for her love:[7]

> For Stella hath with words where faith doth shine,
> Of her high heart given me the monarchy:
> I, I, oh I may say that she is mine,
> And though she give but thus conditionally
> This realm of bliss, while virtuous course I take,
> No kings be crowned, but they some covenants make.

While Sidney's sonnet is wholly positive, deploying metaphorically the language of power and status to suggest his own abjection in face of Stella's conventional Petrarchan power, the poet of Shakespeare's sonnet is deprived – "wanting" – in an insistently financial way. Sidney, of course, could afford such gestures: an aristocrat of the family of the Earls of Pembroke with a family seat at Penshurst, the fantasy of giving a woman power over him was one he could safely indulge.

Not so for Shakespeare, who had to rely not only on his literary skills but also on his entrepreneurial ones to survive and thrive in the competitive bustle of the capital. In Sonnet 87, the youth is the poet's patron, and there is an indelible economic hierarchy inscribed in that relationship which no fantasy can overturn. The poet lacks the noble parts of his fair friend, and the consequences are as much material and legal as they are emotional:

> The cause of this fair gift in me is wanting,
> And so my patent back again is swerving.
> Thy self thou gav'st, thy own worth then not knowing,
> Or me to whom thou gav'st it, else mistaking,
> So thy great gift upon misprision growing,
> Comes home again, on better judgment making.
>> Thus have I had thee as a dream doth flatter,
>> In sleep a king, but waking no such matter.
>
> (87.7–14)

This sonnet implies also the poet's renunciation of his claims to exclusivity with the young man. This is not necessarily sexual exclusivity but the kind of much coveted intimate, privileged access inferiors sometimes had to their social betters, or indeed, more obviously, exclusive patronage. The result of the poet's lack of financial and personal substance is that his monopoly or "patent" on the youth expires. Patents were royal licenses to monopolize the manufacturing or sale of particular commodities for a fixed period of time. Because of the widespread abuse of monopolies and consequent inflationary effect upon prices, the Statute of Monopolies abolished the worst of these practices in 1624 (see Kyle). This monopoly was bestowed upon the poet in error, he claims, before the young man truly knew his own worth or really knew the poet.

The financial and emotional reckoning of this poem is also mirrored in its "numbers," its feminine rhymes. Every line except line 2's "estimate" and line 4's "determinate" has eleven rather than ten syllables, with the last syllable unstressed, as in the "ing" and "er" endings. Only Sonnet 20, "A woman's face with nature's own hand painted," a poem about the youth's ambiguous sexual identity, is also composed of so many feminine rhymes. The use of them in 87 is equally deliberate. The young man is behaving exactly like a capricious Petrarchan mistress who spurns the poet, the only difference being that the poet's ruin is as much economic as it is emotional. Like the chaste Petrarchan lady too, the young man does not spurn the poet because he prefers his rivals, either in love or in poetry, but simply because he has the power to do so.

From the Petrarchan formula of love, interminable desire, dissatisfaction, and deferral, Shakespeare shifts to the experience of love via the economic configuration of scarcity and dearth, where use, exchange, and accumulation – the mechanisms of capitalism – were forces that reconfigured poetry as well. Counting "numbers" had never been more significant.

CHAPTER 6

Time

Whatever worries the poet may have in the dark lady sonnets, time is not one of them. Yet, it is an obsessive theme in the first 126 poems dedicated to the young man. The poet is not at all interested in the woman's biological clock, despite his obsession with the young man's, even though presumably the youth could defer marriage until later in life and still produce a legitimate heir. What, then, makes the poet so concerned about time in relation to the young man and so unconcerned about it in relation to the woman? It is, to paraphrase the Rolling Stones, that time is on his side. However, as the poet repeatedly emphasizes, this is a very temporary state of affairs, and the youth has much to lose (his extraordinary and inherently fragile beauty) to the attrition of age, as well as to other unpredictable forms of change wrought by time's progress. Thus even from the youth's position of unusual advantage, time for him will eventually and invariably run out. The woman, on the other hand, possessed of neither youth nor beauty, has nothing to lose.

Shakespeare's treatment of time in the sonnets essentially rehearses fundamentally Ovidian themes, namely the progress of mutability, loss, grief, and death that constitute the central themes of Ovid's great mythic work, the *Metamorphoses*. In Ovid, metamorphosis is the mythic equivalent of the movement, the shifts and changes that occur over the course of time, to bring about decay, death, and, ultimately, the disintegration of form that is the fate of all organic matter. The changes Ovid describes invariably involve a diminished rather than enhanced human identity – healthy and attractive young people are regularly turned into plants and animals, far less glorious renditions of their former selves.

The argument of this chapter is that in the sonnets time serves as both the instigator and the agent of the common metamorphoses of life, namely age and death. Further, I will argue that while these changes clearly constitute the overriding concerns of the young man sonnets, in relation to the woman there is, paradoxically, no time-driven change, only the stasis of enduring dissatisfaction.

Young Man's Time

"Reckoning time" runs out for the young man in the last poem addressed to him. Although the "boy" begins the poem with time not only on his side but actually in his hand, "in thy power, / Dost hold Time's fickle glass," this is a "sonnet" that falls two lines short of the standard for the genre. Sonnet 126 is thus a twelve-line poem of rhymed couplets that itself runs out before its fourteen lines are up. Nature's bill must be paid, that is, the incipient mortality inherent in every living thing must come: "Her audit, though delayed, answered must be." Lest the reader simply not notice that the poem is short by two lines, the Quarto adds two sets of brackets as if to emphasize the gap created by the missing lines. Sonnet 126 serves as the *envoy* or farewell to the preceding poems to the young man; it offers a final statement on the nature of the poet's relationship with the youth and of the depth of the poet's feeling, which in this instance is the depth of grief at the anticipation of inevitable loss. The reference, which has made many readers uneasy, to the beloved youth as a "boy " – the only such reference in the whole of the Quarto – rather than being indicative of the poet's penchant toward pedophilia, serves to emphasize his youth, that is, the considerable extent of his current credit with time:

> O thou my lovely boy who in thy power,
> Dost hold Time's fickle glass his fickle hour:
> Who hast by waning grown, and therein show'st,
> Thy lovers withering, as thy sweet self grow'st.
> If Nature (sovereign mistress over wrack)
> As thou goest onwards still will pluck thee back,

> She keeps thee to this purpose, that her skill
> May time disgrace, and wretched minutes kill.
> Yet fear her O thou minion of her pleasure,
> She may detain, but not still keep her treasure!
>   Her audit (though delayed) answered must be,
>   And her quietus is to render thee.

The "fickle hour" of line 2 echoes the lament of Sonnet 33, "But out alack, he was but one hour mine," that Michael Wood has claimed, on the basis of a potential pun on "sun" and "son," refers not only to the betrayals of the young man but also to the loss of Shakespeare's son Hamnet, who died in 1585 when he was only 11 years old. Sonnet 33 is about the progression and the loss of "glorious morning" in a cloudy morn:

> Even so my sun one early morn did shine
> With all triumphant splendour on my brow;
> But out alack, he was but one hour mine,
> The region cloud hath masked him from me now.
>   (33.9–12)

Whether or not Sonnet 33's address to the youth is overshadowed by Shakespeare's own paternal grief, the poet's faith in the powers of human reproduction to stave off time is remarkable given the high mortality rates of Elizabethan England. Indeed, the "fickle hour" of Sonnet 126 poignantly suggests not only the inevitability but also, perhaps, the imminence of mortality and thus of the final and permanent separation of the young man from the poet. The time pressure on human reproduction is, therefore, insistent, as in Sonnet 77, "Thou by thy dial's shady stealth mayst know / Time's thievish progress to eternity" (77.7–8). Time is "thievish" not because it is slow but because its progress is clandestine and its movements imperceptible, whether looking at the clock face or at one's own: "Thy dial how thy precious minutes waste" (77.2). Although the passage of time is both inevitable and rapid, the poet makes no argument for surrendering to temporal inevitability, or the graceful acceptance of the progress of growth and the change of seasons. The progress of time is not stately and orderly as in classical and medieval models of time, but careening, so that youth and beauty come crashing into oblivion. This is because the changes brought by nature and time resemble the sudden and startling transformations of Ovid: one minute a beautiful young woman is fleeing the lascivious grasp of Jove, and the next she has become a tree.

Throughout the sonnets, like all mortals the young man owes what is imagined as a debt. Time does not in these sonnets proceed at a steady, constant rate. Like interest compounded on a loan, the debt to time increases. While the general run of humanity also owe their lives to death and must pay up at the end of their allotted span, in the young man's case the debt incurred by his extraordinary beauty is much greater. The consequent pressure of time's acceleration, however, only serves to intensify his fleeting loveliness. Sonnet 18, which unusually refers to a specific calendar month, May, is optimistic that poetry can salvage the young man's beauty from the remorseless progress of time toward death:

> But thy eternal summer shall not fade,
> Nor lose possession of that fair thou ow'st,
> Nor shall Death brag thou wand'rest in his shade,
> When in eternal lines to time thou grow'st.
> (Sonnet 18.9–12)

The conjunction "But" serves to qualify the previous eight lines, which have shown that all nature's beauty is subject to mutability, which manifests as violence, such as the "rough winds" that "shake the darling buds of May" (line 3), accident ("chance," line 7), and decay. "Ow'st" in line 10 serves both as a contraction of "own'st" (referring back to "possession") and "owest," as in that which you owe because you are now in possession of it.

As we saw in the previous chapter, time in the sonnets is figured as an accounts clerk who is always counting, the "reckoning Time" of Sonnet 115, always adding up the moments of life. In 115, Shakespeare explores the paradox that despite time's destruction, it is also the medium of love's growth. The pithy, almost metaphysical logic of this sonnet is not unlike advertisements that promise that faithful application of the product will make the purchaser look years younger in six months. The opening philosophical proposition is that because everything changes with time and always has the potential to change irrevocably for the worse, it would seem reasonable for the poet to claim that his most recent expression of love for the young man is also its fullest. However, earlier poems professing exactly such sentiments as these are now reduced to the status of lies because they are no longer true to the latest flowering of his passion. On these grounds, the poet rejects the opportunity to seize the certainty of the present moment, and cleverly appropriates instead time's propensity toward change by declaring the potential for love's further growth: "Love is a babe: then might I not say so, / To give full growth to that which still doth grow." This is an idea also explored in Sonnet 5, where time destroys the very things that it has so painstakingly brought into being:

> Those hours that with gentle work did frame
> The lovely gaze where every eye doth dwell
> Will play the tyrants to the very same
>
> (5.1–3)

Having manufactured the young man's beauty, time will now set about its destruction, and notably, these lines suggest the caprice of tyranny, of a sudden and unanticipated strike in contrast with the earlier, careful, and therefore slower process of creation. This sense of time's capricious strike is also present in Sonnet 115, where there is an ostensibly objective statement about the effects of time on human life:

> But reckoning time, whose millioned accidents
> Creep in 'twixt vows, and change decrees of kings,
> Tan sacred beauty, blunt the sharp'st intents,
> Divert strong minds to the course of altering things
>
> (115.5–8)

Human agency is here evacuated in favor of time, whose designs force the hand even of the most powerful of mortals ("kings"). Vow breaking, sunburn, failure to execute intentions, all are attributable to exigent circumstances presented by time. Here, as in all the sonnets, time's accelerated progress ultimately distorts beauty in the course of the life span into such grotesque forms that the young man and the poet are confronted with the abrupt and horrifying – the confounding – transformation from youth to decay: "For never resting time leads summer on, / To hideous winter and confounds him there" (5.5–6). "Led on" to his destruction – the reader following across the now perilous precipice that is the enjambment of lines 5 and 6 – the young man is literally misled, but also enticed and seduced by summer, only to be confounded by winter, who again in Sonnet 6 is set to desecrate the young man's beauty: "Then let not winter's ragged hand deface / In thee thy summer." The *threat* of winter carries strong connotations of sexual threat, and the young man's "confounding" bears a resemblance to sexual violation. Summer personified, the young man is "led on," that is, he makes an initial misjudgment at the critical moment that offered his only opportunity for resistance. Ovidian rape not infrequently involves Jove chasing down his prey, but there are also instances of the now obsolete notion of "rape" as abduction (as in the "rape" of Europa, who is carried out to sea by Jove disguised as a milk-white bull), that is, the sense of being swept away. The ravages of time, too, constitute a species of rape, carrying off and overpowering both the beauty and the will of its victim.

Poet's Time

What is striking about the sonnets is that even where their preoccupation with time is most intense, namely in the young man sonnets, it is represented without any chronological specificity whatsoever. We learn only that three years have passed since the poet first met the youth – "Three winters colde," "three summer's pride," "three April perfumes," "three hot Junes" (104.3, 4, 7) – and even this duration in part reflects a lyrical commonplace to be found in Horace, as well as among the Renaissance sonneteers, the French poets Pierre de Ronsard and Philippe Deportes, as well as Shakespeare's English contemporary, Samuel Daniel. As we saw in chapter 1, this absence of dates, days, and so on offers a marked contrast with Petrarch's *Canzoniere*, where one of the most poignant ways the poet registers how loving Laura has changed (and indeed ruined) him is that he remembers the Good Friday he first saw her on April 6, 1327. Shakespeare, on the other hand, gives us no time-frame other than the very abstract and generalized categories of the seasons, seasonal change, and periods of duration, that is, "days," "hours," "minutes, "brief minute[s]," but, notably, not seconds, which had not yet been invented as a temporal designation. This absence of specific chronology, however, does not mean that time runs slowly. On the contrary, the pace of the sonnets is one of "continual haste" (123.12), a tempo Shakespeare owes much more to Ovid, especially to the brisk Latin hexameters of the *Metamorphoses*, than he does to Petrarch. The sense of time in the sonnets, then, derives not from the temporality of the calendar but from what Horace called the *vitae summa brevis*, the short span of human life. However, for Shakespeare, unlike Horace, such inevitable temporal progression is not to be accepted with equanimity. Rather, time, nearly always personified, must be fought off because he actively menaces beauty and love. Time seeks to desecrate beauty with old age and to destroy love by separating the lover from the beloved in death. The poet resists scythe-swinging time every step of the way, and the weapons in this war are biological reproduction and poetry.

While the poet cannot finally dictate, despite his best efforts, whether or not the youth will have children, he can control his "pow'rful rhyme" (55.2). Poetry is claimed as that which will preserve beauty and youth, while the enemy time will destroy it.

The poet achieves some triumphant victories in this battle, as here in Sonnet 19:

> Yet do thy worst, old Time; despite thy wrong,
> My love shall in my verse ever live young
> (19.13–14)

The poet's heroism is always exercised on behalf of the young man, and it is through the power of poetry that conquest is accomplished: "You live in this, and dwell in lovers' eyes" (55.14). But if poetry can achieve indestructibility, the poet himself cannot. He ponders aging in Sonnet 73 as the embers of his soon to be extinguished life: "In me thou seest the glowing of such fire / That on the ashes of his youth doth lie" (73.9–10); and in Sonnet 32, the poet also imagines himself dead, "When that churl death my bones with dust shall cover" (32.2), and wonders what the fate of his poetry will be: "These poor rude lines of thy deceased lover" (32.4). One of the most poignant sonnets in the Quarto is Sonnet 71, whose number reflects the "threescore and ten" years allotted to man's life and anticipates the youth surviving the poet's death. Although it has been read cynically by some recent editors as narcissistic, smug, and insincere (Booth, 1977, 257; Kerrigan, 263), this sonnet conveys the paradox of wishing to be remembered by the beloved while wishing him to be free from the anguish of grief:

> . . . I love you so
> That I in your sweet thoughts would be forgot
> If thinking on me then should make you woe.
>
> (71.6–8)

In Sonnet 64, a geological perception of time, "I have seen the hungry ocean gain / Advantage on the kingdom shore, / And the firm soil win of the wat'ry main" (64.5–7), is brought up short against the sharp emotional realization "That Time will come and take my love away" (64.12). Initial rational observation capitulates to heart-rending recognition, and in the final couplet the poet admits that the lyrical utterance is itself a proleptic response to loss:

> This thought is as a death, which cannot choose
> But weep to have that which it fears to lose.

In contrast to the large-scale effects of time envisaged in Sonnet 64, mechanical, clock time also makes its appearance in the sonnets. In Sonnet 77, as we have seen, Shakespeare draws an analogy between the sundial, the antiquated mechanism of measuring time, and the new "cold, mechanical, inexorable"[1] face of time, the face of the clock, "the dial," and the aging human face, also colloquially known as a "dial." Thus, in "When I have seen by time's fell hand defaced," the opening line of Sonnet 64, the "fell hand" means, of course, cruel hand and refers to the figure of time, who was typically represented with his scythe ready to deliver its descending blow, and in Renaissance emblem books is often equipped, as the young man is in Sonnet 126, with an hourglass. However, "fell hand" is now also the descending hand of the clock, which in Mercutio's joke in *Romeo and Juliet* is on the upswing: "[T]he bawdy hand of the dial is now upon the prick of noon" (*Romeo and Juliet*, 2.4.91–2). The allusion to the descending hand on the dial of a clock is also apparent in the final word of that line, "defaced," containing the word "face," as in "face of the clock," and meaning both to strike down, connoted by "fell," and to strike out or delete.

Notably, two of the poems most keenly concerned with time in Shakespeare's sequence are given symbolically significant numbers: Sonnet 12 is about the twelve hours on the clock face, while Sonnet 60 reflects "our minutes" (60.2):

When I do count the clock that tells the time,
And see the brave day sunk in hideous night;
When I behold the violet past prime,
And sable curls, all silvered o'er with white;
When lofty trees I see barren of leaves,
Which erst from heat did canopy the herd,
And summer's green all girded up in sheaves,
Borne on the bier with white and bristly beard,
Then of thy beauty do I question make,
That thou among the wastes of time must go,
Since sweets and beauties do themselves forsake
And die as fast as they see others grow;
   And nothing 'gainst Time's scythe can make defence
   Save breed to brave him when he takes thee hence.

While the strokes of the scythe refer to an ancient image of death derived from the manual labor of the harvest time, the clock bespeaks mechanical time, and the alliterative monosyllables of the first line count out the ticking of a clock. Counting by the clock is simultaneously the precise record of time and its complete abstraction, while the organic register of temporality is akin to the medieval rhythm of abundance and scarcity, and of time on a human scale and the dignified ritual of death. The last, heavily alliterative line of the octave (Booth, 1971, 75), which John Keats regarded as an aesthetic lapse, forges in fact a deliberate metrical connection with the kind of archaic, mnemonic verse of a world dominated by agricultural labor, the remnant of the language and lyricism of medieval, and even Anglo-Saxon, temporality. This archaic view of time survived in popular images of both the Seven Ages of Man and of the seasons, whose remnants are found in alliterative and even visually alliterative moments of lyric like "Then let not **w**inter's **w**ragged hand deface / In thee thy summer" (6.1–2), as it was originally printed in the Quarto. Most practically and instrumentally, however, this well-nigh obsolete temporality survived in Shakespeare's England in the legal fictions wrought in an effort to secure land tenure in perpetuity. For example, in April 1564, the month of Shakespeare's birth, Solomon Saunders sold a lease for 2,995 years; Thomas Sharpham purchased a lease in Devon until AD 3607; and the property John Hodge's family bought was on a lease that ran out in AD 4609.[2] Such contracts are of the order of the "dateless bargain to engrossing death" made by the lovers in *Romeo and Juliet* and the "doom and date" (line 14) of Sonnet 14. Yet they bespeak a temporality that is no longer the reality of Shakespeare's England, where "reckoning time" (115.5) asserts its demands even on the most privileged members such as Shakespeare's young man.

Woman's Time

Time and change, as we have noted, are *not* controlling themes in the dark lady sonnets, and personified Time does not appear in them despite being an imposing figure in the earlier part of the Quarto. Admittedly, the poet expresses fears about one of time's metamorphoses, namely aging: "my days are past the best" (line 6) in Sonnet 138, "When my love swears that she is made of truth," a poem first published in *The Passionate Pilgrim* when Shakespeare was 35. However, the focus of this sonnet is not so much on getting older as on the mendacity of the woman who pretends to believe his lies (or at least misrepresentations) about his age. In Sonnet 146, addressed to the poet's own soul, time is registered in the expression of anxieties about the "hours of dross" (146.11) that may purchase his everlasting perdition.

In the earlier sonnets, life *is* change and the challenge to be met in it is the kind of constancy or permanence within change that the poet envisaged in Sonnet 116, where love "is an ever fixed mark" (116.5), or in Sonnet 55 where "Nor marble, nor the gilded monuments / Of princes shall outlive this powerful rhyme" (55.1–2). The woman, in contrast, is associated with inconstancy, disease, and death and with the absence of temporal progression:

> Th'expense of spirit in a waste of shame
> Is lust in action: and till action, lust
> Is perjured, murderous, bloody, full of blame,
> Savage, extreme, rude, cruel, not to trust;
> Enjoyed no sooner but despised straight.
> (Sonnet 129.1–5)

In Sonnet 129, the woman's uterus (one of the meanings of the pun on waste/waist) is itself hell. "[T]his hell" (129.14), the very final words of the sonnet, is the place where semen is discharged, and in the terms of the multifaceted meanings of this sonnet, it is both disposed of *and* wasted. Line 3 catalogs not only the nature of this woman, but also in a sense the fetid moral contents of her womb and the evils the poet associates with it. Time and its changes are not in operation: here, nothing grows. This is striking in contrast with the "unear'd [not yet fruitful] womb" (Sonnet 3.5) the young man is enjoined to inseminate: "Make sweet some vial; treasure thou some place" (6.3). This womb, unlike that of the poet's mistress, would hold the sweetness and treasure the young man had carefully bestowed there for safe keeping rather than squandered or discarded as in Sonnet 129. In contrast to the woman's death-dealing womb, something generative could occur here as it does in Sonnet 5. There, the womb is imaged as a glass receptacle: "summers distillation left / A liquid prisoner pent in walls of glasse." For the womb in the young man sonnets is where time (personified) does his creative work. This is the beneficent aspect of time, whose malevolent aspect is time the destroyer:

> Those hours that with gentle work did frame
> The lovely gaze where every eye doth dwell
> (5.1–2)

The gentle work on the embryonic young man was also done in "walls of glass," that is, in the pure, crystalline womb of his mother. The mistress's womb, in contrast, more closely resembles Othello's description: "a cistern for foul toads to knot and [en]gender in" (4.2.61).

If, then, reproductive time is not operative in the woman's womb, what *is* the connection with time? Katherine Duncan-Jones has suggested that the twenty-eight sonnets devoted to the dark lady deliberately correspond with the length of the menstrual cycle (Duncan-Jones, 1997, 99). This coincidence with the duration of "woman's time" is an appropriate structure for the visceral repugnance, what is tantamount to gynephobia, that is the revulsion directed at the organs of female reproduction that the poet expresses throughout these sonnets. In view of the homoerotic thrust of the majority of the sonnets, "Th'expense of spirit in a waste of shame" suggests that expending semen on a woman, let alone *such* a woman, is an improvident use of resources. Of course, there is no reference to "woman," or anyone as such, in the sonnet, which is entirely devoid of personal pronouns. Sonnet 129 tells instead a troubled story of male lust and female reproductive organs. Thus it is not so much the woman or the relationship which is "perjured, murderous, bloody, full of blame," but the womb itself, the site where what was known in the period as the "generative spirit," semen, was ejaculated (Kerrigan, 357).

"Murderous" and "bloody" are typically read by editors as the generalized and abstract evils, killing and brutality, but there are also connotations of the pervasive Renaissance association of womb and tomb as parallel and oddly analogous receptacles for the body and the womb blooded by defloration or menstruation that Shakespeare explores in *Titus Andronicus* and in *Romeo and Juliet*: "[W]hat blood is this which stains / The stony entrance of this sepulcher?" (5.3.140–1). Culturally, the womb, and by extension the evils that androcentric thinking projected onto the feminine, became associated with death and putrefaction. Worn down by the very "lust in action" Sonnet 129 speaks about, the whores in *Pericles*, for example, are described as being "with continual action . . . even as good as rotten" (Kerrigan, 357). In the 1609 Quarto, the line is spelt and punctuated so as to suggest also "full of blood": "*perjured, murderous, blouddy full of blame,*" placing the emphasis of the line syntactically on "*blouddy.*" "Bloody" (129.3) thus carries connotations of menstrual blood, but nor is it far from the *bloody murders* recounted in the period's popular pamphlet literature, such as *A narrative of the bloody murders . . . done in Lincolnshire, made known in 1604*. In addition, this was also a period in which infanticide was vigorously prosecuted, so that the idea of the murdering mother, who kills the offspring of her own womb, may not be too far away in the sonnet.

While gynephobia might be expected of Sonnet 129, it is more surprising to find the poet praising the young man because he is not subject to *woman's time* and does not menstruate in Sonnet 18, "Shall I compare thee to a summer's day." Here the reference to the idea that the youth's beauty is not subject to the processes of "nature's changing course" in line 8 bespeaks the fact that the youth's beauty is not regularly interrupted and set off-balance by what were known in the period as "monthly courses" (Duncan-Jones, 1997, 47).

Even without comparison to Sonnet 18, the tenor of Sonnet 129 is indeed startling. It is possible that "Th'expense of spirit" is the rhetorical equivalent of the considerable violence directed at prostitutes in early modern London. The Victorian critic William Minto, writing in 1874, argued that the twenty-eight sonnets concerning the dark lady were "addressed to a courtesan" (Rollins, II, 253). The feminist response came as early as 1923 when Helene Richter argued that in the dark lady sonnets, "Shakespeare goes far beyond conventional anti-Petrarchanism and is cold-blooded to the point of cruelty" (Rollins, II, 252).

*

The poet does not seek liberation from the vicissitudes of time on his own behalf. Rather, all his resistances to time are aimed at the preservation of the youth. It is the young man who is the living embodiment of beauty, and at once represents the poet's highest ideals and epitome of human vulnerability to time's relentless yet almost imperceptible passing: "Ah, yet doth beauty, like a dial hand, / Steal from his figure, and no pace perceived" (104.91–10). One of the ironies of the sonnets is that the twenty-eight poems about the woman "colored ill" have survived the ravages of time just as well as those addressed to the picture-perfect young man.

Appendix: The Matter
of the Sonnets

There is no question that close examination of the sonnets reveals a plethora of rhetorical figures, of which the following set is a far from exhaustive list: *repetition* (for example, 99.2); *anaphora*, the repetition of a word or expression at the beginning of successive phrases for rhetorical or poetic effect (18.13–14); *traductio* (Latin) or *polyptoton*, a figure of speech in which a word is repeated in a different form of the same root or stem, or repeated with its word class changed into a different part of speech (82.11–12); *anadiplosis* (from the Greek "doubled back"), the repetition of a prominent (usually the final) word of a phrase, clause, line, or stanza at the beginning of the next, often with extended or altered meaning (129.8–9); *antiphrasis*, saying one thing while meaning the opposite, sometimes distinguished from *ironia* or irony (94); *paradiastole* or excusing, or what George Puttenham in *The Arte of English Poesie* calls "Curry-favel" (35, 42, 129). Early modern texts like Puttenham's, as well as Thomas Wilson's *The Art of Rhetorique* and Henry Peacham's *The Garden of Eloquence*, all addressed the technical matter of rhetoric.

In contrast to this emphasis, however, Douglas Peterson, in *The English Lyric From Wyatt to Donne*, persuasively argues that despite the prevalence of rhetoric and prosody, the best English poetry was primarily concerned with "matter," or content (Peterson, 6). Indeed, poetry was also understood to be much more than either verse form or technical accomplishment by Sir Philip Sidney, who famously draws the distinction in the *Apology for Poetry* (1583) between "verse," which he defines as "an ornament and no cause to Poetry," and true poetry: "It is already said (and, as I think, truly said) it is not rhyming and versing that maketh Poesie. One may be a Poet without versing, and a versifier without Poetry" (quoted Steele, 140). What is it, then, that "maketh poetry" in Shakespeare's sonnets if it is not simply their verse form? The answer to that question is invariably complex, but in its broadest outlines it is the convergence of form and meaning, which this appendix will endeavor to elucidate.

While sonnets cannot and should not be *reduced* to their paraphrasable content, it remains important to ascertain the nature of that content, which is frequently of some surprising logical and narrative complexity. The content of the sonnets is, in addition, especially important in terms of the key questions about whether the order of the sonnets in the first Quarto is that of a sequence – a progressive ordering – or a collection – a more arbitrary anthology of lyrics whose unifying element is their sonnet form rather than their linear coherence. Clearly, the sonnets do not follow a lock-step pattern of narrative progression, but if the poems are indeed autobiographical, they may reflect the structure of memory, the mental impression of real events rather than linear time. Eudora Welty's remarks on the writer's processing of life events is pertinent here: "The events in our life happen in a sequence in time, but in their significance to ourselves they find their own order, a timetable not necessarily – perhaps not possibly – chronological. The time as we know it subjectively is often the chronology that stories and novels follow: it is a continuous thread of revelation" (Welty, 94). Yet, in the (probably erroneous) belief that Shakespeare did not authorize publication of the Quarto, numerous attempts have been made over the years to claim a different order for the sonnets than the one presented in the Quarto. My commentary, on the contrary, will strive to demonstrate the often fluid continuity between one sonnet and another without trying to force the sonnets into a definitive pattern or into the more rigid parameters of a formal sequence.

Thinking about the sonnets in this way also provokes the question about whether they are indeed addressed to only one woman and one man. The man is certainly of unimpeachable virtue in some sonnets, while in others he takes a tumble from his pedestal to fall into the realms of all-too-human moral frailty. Human beings are of course composed of a range of character traits, both good and bad, and one person could possess all the qualities that Shakespeare ascribes to the youth. However, the poet gives up rather abruptly on the project of begging the young man to marry, either because the youth does so – though if he does, no further mention is made of his progeny – or because the poet is now addressing someone else. This lack of explanation and the absence of specific information intensify the sense that the sonnets refer to an internal world of emotion and relationship, on which the externals of names, dates, and historical events intrude very rarely, as for instance in Sonnet 107, in what is potentially an oblique reference to the death of Elizabeth. What *is* definitive is that "I always write of you" (Sonnet 76.9). While we may not be able to determine the identity of the "I" or the "you" at any point in the sequence, it is this fundamental dynamic that constitutes the essential cohesiveness of the sonnets: the engagement of the poet's "I" with the "you" he addresses. What occupies the thinking and the argument of the sonnets is always the poet's relationship with a significant other, and it is this relationship that determines his perspective on his life and on the nature of time, beauty, and mortality.

The sonnets do not, then, have a plot like a novel, but they do have a strong and intriguing narrative element that absorbs the reader all the more for not fully disclosing the persons and events to which they refer. The lack of factual evidence and information is not, however, simply meant to tantalize the reader like the missing clue of a detective novel (although too many critics have treated the sonnets as precisely a more literary brand of detective fiction). Rather, the absence of all information extraneous to the poet's feelings about his relationships gives the reader a window on his interior life, so that we seem to be looking with his eyes out at the beloved and inward to his own mind and heart. In this, Shakespeare replicates the texture of intimacy: we cannot get any more up close and personal than this.

While the sonnets do not have a conventional narrative, then, many of them do have an argument, and the thought of each sonnet is frequently structured in a Petrarchan movement of the octave giving way to the sestet. The shadow of the Italian sonnet generates the sonnets' lyrical energy, just as the final couplet complicates that structure even in offering a formal resolution to it.

Sonnet 1

Proposing that nature inclines toward the perpetuation and increase of what is beautiful, in the opening sonnet the youth is charged with unnatural behavior in selfishly hoarding himself. The poet urges him instead to take pity on the world and bear children. Failure to do so makes him guilty of self-consuming narcissism and deserving of the extinction that will then be his lot.

Sonnet 2

Shakespeare here adapts a traditional argument for procreation commonly used in poems whose aim was the seduction of a woman. In this sonnet, the poet urges that instead of simply losing his beauty, the young man should confer that beauty on a child.

Sonnet 3

Here the youth is enjoined to look at his face in the mirror, to view its youthfulness and become aware that it is time to have children. His beauty is such that any woman would desire his children, and in reproducing his beauty and image will be perpetuated, just as he perpetuates the youthful beauty of his own mother whom he so much resembles. The alternative is a funeral monument to his self-love and the termination of his lineage. His beauty will thus remain in the world even as old age wizens his features. The concluding threat is that failure to reproduce means that his beauty dies with him.

Sonnet 4

In a series of pointed interrogatives, the poet asks why the youth squanders the legacy of his beauty on himself instead of investing it with nature by procreating. The poet accuses the young man of miserliness, and of engaging in the evils of usury without reaping its financial rewards. The natural conclusion of the young man's life will see his beauty interred with him, unless he uses his beauty to bear children.

Sonnet 5

Time in its creative aspect has fashioned the young man's beauty, but time does not stop, and inevitably, age and death await him. The only insurance against this fate is to preserve beauty in the way that the process of distillation preserves flowers. The analogy is a specifically sexual one whereby the young man's seminal substance is preserved in the receptive vessel of the woman's womb.

Sonnet 6

The poet pleads with the young man not to let winter destroy his beauty before it has been preserved by distillation. He begs that the youth impregnate someone, assuring him that, unlike the practice of usury, it is not morally wrong to reproduce, but, echoing the language of the parable of the talents in the New Testament, that this is legitimate increase. The poet further assures the young man that his life would endure in his offspring even after his own demise, while the couplet threatens that by failing to bequeath his beauty to posterity, only the worms in his grave will inherit it.

Sonnet 7

This sonnet compares the progress of the personified sun through the heavens to the course of the young man's life. Like the sun, he may be worshipped even in middle age, but in old age, formerly loyal admirers will avert their gaze from him. The final couplet, with its pun on "son" and "sun" in which the analogy is made explicit, threatens that the youth will die in obscurity if he does not have a son.

Sonnet 8

The poet continues to enjoin the young man to marry and reproduce but in rather less menacing tones than in the preceding sonnets. Asking the young man why he takes pleasure in listening to sad music, the poet suggests that it is because the music gently reprimands him for persisting in the unharmonious, unmarried state. The concord of the strings of an instrument is like that of a happy family, in contrast to the youth's sterile, single state.

Sonnet 9

The tone of this sonnet shifts again to ponder the world after the youth's demise. The poet begins asking the young man if he remains single because he would not want to make his wife a widow. The question seems benign enough, because it presupposes that compassion motivates the young man to remain a bachelor. However, the query also assumes the inevitability of the youth's untimely demise. The poet urges that even if the youth dies single, the world will be his grieving widow devoid of even the consolation of having children who resemble her dead spouse. Thus, squandering beauty is more reprehensible even than wasting money because at least money remains in circulation after it is spent. The couplet charges the youth with both self-love and self-murder.

Sonnet 10

The poet harps on the young man's selfish, self-destructive narcissism. This time he accuses him of being both murderous and hateful, and in an analogy between a house, a family seat, and the youth's body he claims that the young man aims to ruin rather than repair it. From the Petrarchan turn at line 9, the poet compares the beautiful exterior of the young man with his hateful heart, to change his mind, principally for his own benefit but also, in a striking note of intimacy, for love of the poet himself.

Sonnet 11

This sonnet takes up again the idea that growth and decay progress at exactly the same rate, allowing progeny to rejuvenate and warm an otherwise senile, decrepit world. The alternative is that the human race would end within sixty years. The poet urges that while those who are physically unprepossessing were not meant to reproduce, the beautiful, in contrast, have a particular duty to procreate, which is figured in the concluding couplet in terms of mechanical rather than biological reproduction, that is, from printing copies off a stamp carefully crafted by a personified Nature.

Sonnet 12

Deliberately positioned so that, as Mercutio puts it, "the bawdy hand of the dial is now upon the prick of noon" (*Romeo and Juliet*); this sonnet contemplates the passing of the hour, the day, and the season from vigor to decay and death. This fate, the poet realizes, will also befall the youth because one beauty fades as another blossoms. The only defense against menacing time is reproduction.

Sonnet 13

Addressing the young man as "love" in the very first line and "dear my love" in the last, this sonnet assumes the type of intimacy apparent in Sonnet 10. Once again, the case for reproduction is presented as a form of moral probity associated with good husbandry, that is, with the proper upkeep of family property, rather than the negligence of spendthrift gentry who let their family seats fall into ruinous disrepair for want of upkeep. Only a prodigal son would behave thus: since the youth had a father, he should maintain beauty, family honor, property, and lineage by becoming a parent himself.

Sonnet 14

Acknowledging he is no astronomer, the poet nonetheless claims predictive powers. Deploying a conventional Petrarchan trope, the poet divines the future by the youth's eyes, the stars in his head, rather than by the stars in the heavens. The prediction is overwhelmingly positive but only if the young man allows his lineage to be saved by siring children. Otherwise, the bleak future holds only the absolute termination of the qualities of truth and beauty currently embodied by the youth.

Sonnet 15

The poet ponders that all living things appear perfectly on the stage of existence only for that single moment, after their maturation and prior to their decay. Like all organic life, human life is mutable, and although now in his youth, the young man's vigor will be wasted by time and decay. In this war with time, the poet can reinvigorate and renew the youth by means of his poetry.

Sonnet 16

This sonnet follows directly on from the argument of the preceding one suggesting that biological reproduction is a surer means of defeating time than poetry. The horticultural imagery continues here also, as the youth's potential children are likened to "flowers," the organic counterpart of "poesy," that is, of the flowers of art. A living child would more accurately render the likeness of the youth than his portrait, either painted or in verse. Neither beauty nor personal merit can make the youth endure. Paradoxically, only in giving himself away to marriage can the youth preserve the integrity of his identity, and his own skill in lovemaking can continue his line.

Sonnet 17

This final sonnet enjoining the youth to procreate argues that the poet's verse will strike succeeding generations as outlandish hyperbole unless there is a living descendant to verify the qualities he now ascribes to him. Further, the poet promises not only that the young man will live on, but that he will live on twice, in his heir and in the poem.

Sonnet 18

This sonnet marks a transition from the procreation sonnets as the poet confidently asserts that the youth will endure forever in these lines of verse. He engages in exactly the kind of poetic hyperbole he had argued was vulnerable to the charge of exaggeration in the preceding sonnet. In 18, all metaphors are inadequate in face of the youth's beauty because they miss the mark of perfection. This sonnet and the ones that follow it may have been written to a different addressee.

Sonnet 19

The dynamic of the relationship changes in the course of the sonnets that follow the plea to procreate. In this and the preceding sonnet, the poet emphasizes the power of poetry to make the young man live forever despite the ravages of "Devouring time."

Sonnet 20

The intimate familiarity with which the speaker addresses the sexually ambiguous young man has made this sonnet the fulcrum of debates about Shakespeare's own sexual identity. The sonnet uses feminine rhymes throughout. The youth looks like a woman and is the object of both male and female admiration. The slippery language of the couplet makes a bawdy pun on the youth's "prick" and renounces at least reproductive sexual relations with him.

Sonnet 21

The next five poems (21–5) perpetuate the ambivalent identity of the addressee, by using no gender pronouns at all in reference to him. Criticizing the vulgar hyperbole used by other poets, albeit in a much milder form than Sonnet 130, this sonnet explores the problem of poetic originality within the conventional tropes of love poetry. Here, in an idea that Shakespeare also explores in *Lucrece*, he posits Petrarchan hyperbole as a form of advertising, the tawdry commodification of something, or rather someone, too precious for sale or advertisement. (Despite these protestations, in Sonnet 24 we will find the image of the beloved on display in a shop.)

Sonnet 22

Since the older poet and his beloved have exchanged hearts, the poet reasons that they must be of the same youthful age. The exchange of hearts is a conventional poetic topos, and here it suggests that there is complete union – sexual as well as emotional – between the speaker and the addressee. This poem also contains one of the two instances in the sonnets where the erotic relationship is figured as that between a mother and child (the other is Sonnet 143).

Sonnet 23

Tongue-tied, the poet fears his ability to express his feelings to the beloved, who induces in him the equivalent of stage fright, or the debilitating excess of passion. At line 9, he argues that the written rather than the spoken word is therefore a more appropriate vehicle for the articulation of his love.

Sonnet 24

One of several references in the sonnets to visual art, this sonnet alludes to the relatively recent advent of perspectival drawing. Suggesting intimate proximity, the sonnet plays upon the idea of looking so closely into the eyes of the lover that one can see one's own image. The Renaissance expression for this was "looking babies into one another's eyes," referring to the miniaturized image (the "baby" version of oneself) reflected in the pupils. The poet's eyes have painted the beloved's image in his heart, where it hangs like a portrait displayed in a painter's shop. In parallel fashion, the image of the speaker in the beloved's eyes is a window to his soul, wherein the lover resides. The couplet, however, strikes a discordant note of distrust whereby the poet and the beloved's hearts remain opaque one to another.

Sonnet 25

The final couplet of this sonnet potentially offers evidence against the theory that the fair youth of the sonnets is someone of considerable fame: "Then happy I that love and am beloved / Where I may not remove nor be removed." For the speaker rejoices that neither he nor his love are in the public eye, like court favorites who can fall from grace and lose everything at any moment. The reference to "The painful warrior" is potentially an allusion to the Earl of Essex, beheaded after his foiled rebellion against Elizabeth, or to the Earl of Southampton, who was imprisoned in the Tower for two years for his role in the plot and stripped of his title.

Sonnet 26

In contrast to the previous sonnets, which have refrained from specifying the gender of the addressee, and to the preceding sonnet, which suggests that the addressee is not of a particularly exalted status, this sonnet, an abject expression of the poet's social and literary unworthiness, opens by addressing him as a male social superior, "Lord of my love," and in the remainder of the poem reveals the yawning chasm of class distinction between them. Yet this poem also deploys feminine rhymes in lines 6, 8, 9–12, 13, and 14. The submissive tone comports with the rhetorical strategy known as "disabling speech," which was, for example, standard practice in parliamentary oratory, whereby the speaker expressed his unworthiness and incapacity, usually as a prelude to a lengthy and carefully eloquent address. This sonnet resembles a dedicatory sonnet more than a love sonnet.

Sonnet 27

This sonnet assumes a very different tone and is written on an entirely more intimate emotional register. The travel-weary speaker goes to bed but gets no sleep there because his mind makes a pilgrimage to the beloved. The decidedly religious image of the addressee as a jewel shining in the darkness summons up the interior of a church. The sense of adoration is, however, tempered by the couplet, which stresses the restless, tormented nature of this love, which compels the poet to relinquish the physical rest and mental "quiet" that he craves. This is the first of five sonnets that explore the conventional Petrarchan themes of night and sleeplessness.

Sonnet 28

The agonies of separation from the addressee take their toll on the poet. There is a narrative and structural continuity between this sonnet and the preceding one, which again addresses the torment of insomnia, a theme Shakespeare took up at length in *Macbeth*. Here, however, it is desire rather than guilt that induces sleeplessness. Exhausted by his work during the day and tortured again with sleeplessness at night, his turmoil is compounded and his grief at separation only intensifies.

Sonnet 29

Tormented now by a gnawing sense of worthlessness and wishing he could change his state with those better-looking, more talented, and well connected, the poet remembers the beloved. This blissful recollection transforms his perception of his life as something so cherished and precious that he would not exchange it for any worldly advantage.

Sonnet 30

The sonnet continues the theme of grief, but while it is a poem about memory, its language is surprisingly legal and financial. The poet meditates in solitude on past sorrows, failures, the memory of deceased friends, financial losses, and on old wounds. The concluding couplet, however, offers the compensation as all woes vanish in recollection of the "dear friend."

Sonnet 31

Continuing the argument of the previous sonnet, the poet claims that all his dead loved ones live now in his "friend" because his present love for the young man encompasses all past loves as well. Similarly, because he is in possession of the poet's love, the young man enjoys the love of anyone the poet has ever loved or anyone who has loved the poet.

Sonnet 32

In the event that the beloved outlives the poet and that his poetry is surpassed by subsequent verse, the poet enjoins the addressee to read the superior verses of others for their stylistic merits and his own poetry for its love, which he suggests is its greatest merit. This sonnet strikes an intimate and vulnerable tone, when the poet imagines himself as "thy deceased lover" and considers the possibility of being overshadowed by greater poets than himself. The latter may indicate Shakespeare's consciousness of his time as that of the greatest age of English poetry.

Sonnet 33

Unlike so many of the preceding sonnets, this one contains quite specifically male pronouns. Drawing out the analogy between the beauty of the sun and the beauty of the beloved, the young man's glory is now obscured by dark clouds. The poet laments this estrangement – a theme that continues through Sonnet 36 – but the couplet asserts his continued love for the young man, reasoning that if the sun in heaven is given license to be "stained," then surely his terrestrial counterpart must be permitted his faults and transgressions.

Sonnet 34

Feeling betrayed by the youth, the poet asks why he has misled him, claiming that he has been shamed by the unspecified error the young man has committed. This sonnet continues the imagery of the sun, whose clouded face has now given way to rain and storm, suggesting that the ills of the relationship have intensified. Even the young man's penitence cannot rectify the wrong he has done the poet, though the couplet accepts the youth's tears as compensation for all the injuries he has suffered. Thus the tone of the poem shifts from that of indignant injury at the start to indulgence at his tears by the end.

Sonnet 35

We learn in this sonnet that the young man is guilty of some "sensual fault." The first quatrain seeks to excuse the fault, while in the second the poet claims that he has been an accessory to the youth's crimes because of his lenience.

Sonnet 36

In the last of the estrangement sonnets, the poet accepts the necessity of separation and does so in the first two lines in language that evokes the marital bond. Somewhat masochistically, he will carry the moral faults of the young man as his own. But as a result of this burden, the poet can no more acknowledge their relationship since doing so would only bring the very shame on the young man that he has just alleviated, and nor can the youth publicly recognize him. This would only be possible if the youth did not have the "name," that is, the social status, perhaps even the aristocratic title, that requires him to sustain his reputation.

Sonnet 37

The opening analogy of this sonnet suggests a paternal relationship with the addressee. Like an old man who takes delight in the vigor of his son, the poet similarly enjoys the wealth, beauty, and prestige of the youth despite having suffered some serious misfortune. The metaphor for this ill-luck suggests that the poet had been crippled in the very essence of his art in being "made lame," a term that resonates with poetry because it is made up of metrical "feet." Once again, however, the poet is compensated with interest for his troubles by the flourishing beauty and excellence of the youth.

Sonnet 38

Extending the notion of being paid back tenfold for his trouble in the previous sonnet, the poet declares that his powers of poetic invention could never be impaired because he writes of the addressee who is his tenth Muse (there are only nine). If he achieves any success in poetry, then the praise is due to the young man who has inspired him.

Sonnet 39

This is the third poem in succession in which the poet has claimed that the youth is his better part. In this sonnet, however, he returns to the theme that the lovers are divided. Such separation affords the opportunity of allowing the poet to praise the youth, which, he reasons, could not occur when they were united as one. The "turn" of the sonnet shifts to a lament for the absent youth, the only consolation for which is the time it affords for "thoughts of love" and for apprehending the paradox of the identity – that the youth has become part of the poet – that results from such profound love.

Sonnet 40

The poet has again suffered a grievance at the hands of the young man, but once again forgives him. On this occasion, the youth's treachery consists in taking one of the poet's "loves" or lovers. This theme occurs again in the woman colored ill sonnets, so that most critics assume that the same situation, namely the love triangle between the youth, the woman, and the poet, is also being referred to here. Editors often emend "this self" of line 7 to "thy self," which also occurs in line 8. Given that 36–9 have explored the entanglements of the poet's identity with the beloved, "this self" may not be a compositor's error but an indication that the youth's behavior is a species of self-deception.

Sonnet 41

Plunging once again into the language of gendered specificity, this sonnet adds a new figure, "the woman," and is more forthcoming with the details of the youth's infidelity. The poet forgives the young man's errors as natural to his youth and beauty. By the Petrarchan "turn" of line 9, however, the poet remonstrates with him for having taken his (implicitly sexual) place with his mistress.

Sonnet 42

The poet's greatest loss is not the woman but the young man. Taking up again the idea that his identity has merged with that of the young man, the poet reasons that the young man loves the woman because the poet loves her, and the woman has appropriated the youth for the sake of the poet. By one mode of reasoning the poet has lost both his loves; by more specious reasoning his mistress loves only him, because he and the youth are one.

Sonnet 43

Addressing another dimension of the theme addressed in Sonnet 27, the poet explores the paradox that night brings the mental vision of the absent youth despite his absence. In the poet's world, turned upside down by the separation from his beloved, closed eyes, sleep, and night bring vision, whereas the daylight offers only blindness and darkness.

Sonnet 44

The poet bemoans the fact that matter, gross physical reality, prevents his reunion with the youth. Thought, in contrast, offers no such impediments, and the poet could fly to him despite distance if "the dull substance" of flesh did not weigh him down. Since he is composed of matter as well as thought, the poet is subject to the laws of time and space and thus must wait and bemoan the absence of the youth.

Sonnet 45

This third consecutive sonnet on the theme of absence continues the preceding sonnet's focus on the constraints of matter. Of the four elements, air and fire represent his immaterial thoughts and desires, which serve as messengers to the absent youth, while the denser elements of earth and water stay behind with the poet and are the cause of his depression. This sonnet also explores the paradox of the presence-absence of the beloved, a theme addressed by Sidney in *Astrophil and Stella* (106.1).

Sonnet 46

Sonnets 46 and 47 explore a conventional conceit about the self-conflicted identity of people in love, which is here figured as an antipathy between the eye and the heart. The debate between the parties is staged as a scene of contentions litigation where the heart is the defendant. The jury who settle the case decide (albeit somewhat cryptically) that the eye has title to the youth's external appearance, and the heart to his inward qualities.

Sonnet 47

Having reached an agreement, the eye and the ear can now console one another with images of the young man. The controlling metaphor up to line 9 is one of consumption, of feeding and banqueting on the youth who is still absent from the poet. Because he is always in his thoughts, the young man remains with him nonetheless.

Sonnet 48

When he left, the poet carefully locked up his valuables, neglecting to safeguard his most cherished jewel, namely the young man. Here as in the preceding sonnets the beloved is contained within the poet's heart and mind, but the poet recognizes regretfully that this is no insurance against actual theft.

Sonnet 49

Although in Sonnet 48 the poet failed to make any preparations to insure against the theft of his beloved, he now turns to anticipate the potential future loss of the young man's love and braces himself for rejection. There can be no legal remedy against the youth's removal of his affections since there are no reasons or legal causes for it (or indeed for the poet's love) in the first place. Both 48 and 49, though critics have sometimes argued that they are out of sequence, in fact address the poet's fears about his relationship with the young man.

Sonnet 50

The poet reluctantly undertakes a journey away from his beloved and once again endures the weight of matter and the subjection to laws of time and space that work only to divide him from the beloved. The horse on which the poet rides – a figure for the poet's own emotionally burdened physicality as well as his emotional torment – seems to empathize with his melancholic disposition, plodding on slowly and groaning when stabbed by his rider's spur. All joy is at the poet-traveler's point of origin, and only grief at his destination.

Sonnet 51

This sonnet makes a pair with the preceding one, and picks up the earlier theme of the enabling elements of air and fire as opposed to earth and water that keep the lovers apart. The horse trudges on away from the beloved, but on the return journey the poet's desire will speed him home as he hopes to transcend the physical limitations of matter, and travel by flying with the speed of fiery desire.

Sonnet 52

In this sonnet, which coincides with the number of weeks in a year, the poet tries to put the best face on the separation from his beloved by arguing that precious things and special occasions must be experienced sparingly lest they become mundane. In imagery heavy with sexual associations, the poet compares himself to someone in possession of a priceless object. Although possessing the key to the treasure chest, the owner refrains from continual viewing lest he blunt his appetite for its beauty. At the Petrarchan turn, the poet reasons that time functions as the locked container that keeps him from the youth, so that he will experience the ecstasy of seeing him again, and while he is without him will eagerly anticipate him.

Sonnet 53

Following the theme of treasure explored in the previous sonnet, and the density of matter confronted in the separation sonnets, Sonnet 53, potentially addressed to beauty itself, poses philosophical questions on a neo-Platonic register about what constitutes beauty. More beautiful than both male and female paragons, the youth both partakes of and lends beauty to everything that exists. Playing on the Platonic distinction between essence (substance) and image (shadow/shape), the poet claims (somewhat surprisingly in view of the sexual treachery that has gone on thus far) that the youth's moral virtues exceed even his unrivaled external attributes.

Sonnet 54

Continuing the theme of the distinction between outer appearance and inner reality, the poet argues that truth intensifies beauty. This sonnet also returns to some of the imagery of roses and perfume from the procreation sonnets, especially Sonnets 5 and 6. The argument veers away from the idealizations of the preceding sonnet, and strikes a cautionary note by warning that dog roses look as good as real ones, but they lack the essence, the perfume of real roses, and so when they die, nothing of them endures. The poet holds off from issuing the kind of threat he made in the procreation sonnets, claiming instead that his poetry distills the youth's essence.

Sonnet 55

Having made his pitch for poetry's capacity to distill the essence of beauty, in the tradition of the poets of antiquity the speaker makes a bold claim for the capacity of his sonnets to outlast time and thus make the young man live forever. The controlling figure is that of the funeral monument and its vulnerability to the depredations of time in spite of its splendor and material solidity.

Sonnet 56

In a sonnet that registers the complexity of human relationships, the poet urges the importance of reviving the former passion of their attachment. Their present separation offers an opportunity to rekindle their formerly ardent feelings for one another. It is unclear as to whether the passion of one or both parties has waned. This sonnet is thematically connected with similar concerns in Sonnet 52 and about blunting the force of desire with over-familiarity.

Sonnet 57

Reading this sonnet upon the preceding one suggests that it is the youth who has gone away. Instead of the heart-felt pining provoked by previous absences, the poet suffers from impatience at having to attend to the conveniences of the youth, especially since he reproaches the youth with suspicions about his behavior. The imagery of this poem invokes both a rigid social hierarchy, positing the youth as "my sovereign" and the poet as "your slave," and a specifically Petrarchan one in which the beloved plays the cruel tyrant to the wretched and servile poet.

Sonnet 58

Like the previous sonnet, this invokes the feudal theme in which the beloved has sovereign power over the abject lover. The tone of disgruntled irony in both poems is that of the slighted servant, a theme whose tragic connotations Shakespeare explored in the character of Iago in *Othello*. The poet waits both for and on the youth, a necessity that torments him. Like a servant, however, the poet is aware that he has no right to question the comings and going of his employer.

Sonnet 59

Presenting an abrupt change in tone, this sonnet returns to the agenda of Sonnet 53 to offer an adequate artistic representation of the impossibly beautiful young man. Since there is nothing new under the sun, the search for poetic novelty involves the futile labor of rebirthing a child who has already been born. In an image that speaks to the Renaissance consciousness about the artistic and literary achievements of classical antiquity, the poet wishes he could indeed see some ancient representation of the youth, so that he could tell whether classical or contemporary art is superior or whether creative developments have come full circle. Certainly, poetic and artistic invention, the poet reasons, must have been spent in the past on more unworthy objects than the young man.

Sonnet 60

The number assigned this sonnet is significant in referring to the number of minutes in the hour. While the previous sonnet pondered great swaths of time from antiquity to the poet's present day, this one contemplates what was, when Shakespeare wrote the sonnets, the smallest unit in which time could be measured. The passage of time brings growth, change, decay, and ultimately death. The poet hopes his record of the youth's qualities will serve as a bulwark against time's implacable progress.

Sonnet 61

Returning to the themes of sleep and dreaming addressed in the separation sonnets, especially Sonnet 43, The poet asks in the octave if the youth has sent his image like a ghost to disturb his sleep because he is jealously suspicious about what the poet might be doing in his absence. The ghost is a particularly pertinent image in the sonnets – it is spirit without matter, and thus the antithesis of the poet's concerns about matter without spirit, which so horrifies him in the depictions of the youth by other poets. The remainder of this sonnet reveals that it is rather the poet's feelings, not the youth's, that induce his insomnia. The young man, the poet imagines, is probably awake somewhere else because he is with "others," someone else.

Sonnet 62

Playing again on the theme of image versus reality and the idea that, despite their physical distinctiveness, the identities of the lover and the beloved are inseparable, the poet now contemplates himself. In his mind's eye, through the octave, he finds himself perfectly acceptable, and even has an idealized image of himself. But looking in the mirror, he sees his face "beaten and chopped" (weather-beaten and lined) with age. In fact, what he praises in himself is his beloved, whose identity he shares because, as we have seen, for example in Sonnets 22 and 48, the youth lives in the poet's heart. Thus, the young man now paints the poet, so he is both depicted and ornamented by the beauty of the youth.

Sonnet 63

Exactly at the halfway mark of the poems to the young man, the poem now reverses the image of the previous sonnet to contemplate a time when the young man will look as aged and worn as the poet does now. The poet claims his poetry is an insurance against this inevitable decay. However, the poet claims, even if time takes the youth's life, he will not take his beauty because it is preserved forever in the poet's verse.

Sonnet 64

The first eleven lines contemplate time and mutability, from whose forces nothing is unaffected. The progress of time is considered not in terms of the *summa brevis* (the brief span), the changes of a single, brief lifetime, but rather the passage of time from age to age in terms of human history, and the progress of time as it is marked on nature, changing the shape of land and sea. All of these changes are considered in terms of their destructive force. At line 12, the poet shifts his meditation to the personal register in a poignant expression of the anticipated loss of the beloved to death.

Sonnet 65

Continuing directly from the argument of the two previous poems, the poet resumes the itinerary of all that is vulnerable to time. In a series of four questions, he asks how time can be stayed and to allow anything to survive. He resorts to the potentially miraculous powers of poetry to preserve his love.

Sonnet 66

This is the poet's death wish whose cause is a series of eleven social injustices presented via the rhetorical figure of repetition known as anaphora, in the repetitions of "And" in ten lines of the sonnet. All that keeps the speaker from death is the thought of leaving his love. The number of this sonnet may be significant, associated with the mark of the beast from the Book of Revelation (13:16–18), and it is a departure from the structure of four quatrains and a couplet that characterizes the Shakespearean sonnet. Line 9, the shadow of the Petrarchan turn, contains one of the most famous lines in Shakespeare, "art made tongue-tied by authority."

Sonnet 67

The poet now shifts the issue of the preceding sonnet from his own desire to die to that of why the young man should live among such corruption. He indicts art – both cosmetic and creative – for its imitation and exploitation of the youth. Bankrupt nature keeps the young man alive only to show her former glories.

Sonnet 68

Making a pair with the preceding sonnet, the poet says that the young man is the only sign of what beauty used to be now that artifice, cosmetics, and wigs offer such shabby imitations. The young man still shows what authentic beauty consists of and is nature's paradigm of what beauty used to be before art became such a degraded imitation of it.

Sonnet 69

In contrast to several of the earlier poems (for example, Sonnet 35) where the poet is at pains to excuse the faults of his friend, the poet now finds the youth morally culpable for the reputation he has begun to acquire. While so many of the sonnets praise the young man's personal and moral qualities, this sonnet points to a disturbing disjunction between the youth's appearance and his reputation and behavior. A foul smell is now beginning to emanate from the fair exterior, caused, so the poet charges, by the unworthy persons with whom the youth has chosen to associate.

Sonnet 70

Shifting from the reproachful tone of the preceding sonnet, the poet now claims that beautiful people are invariably the subject of slanderous gossip. This sonnet suggests that time has now passed, that the young man is no longer so young because he has "passed the ambush of young days," that is, the period when he would have been particularly vulnerable to those vices that entrap young people. The couplet urges that if it were not for slander, the addressee would be universally adored.

In relation to the preceding sonnet, this is a poem of forgiveness and its number, seventy, may echo the passage from Matthew's gospel where Jesus is asked about the limits of Christian mercy in terms of multiples of seven: "Then came Peter to him, and said, Lord, how oft shall my brother sin against me, and I forgive him? till seven times? Jesus saith unto him, I say not unto thee, Until seven times: but, Until seventy times seven" (Matthew 18:22–3).

Sonnet 71

The next four sonnets contemplate the beloved addressee living on after his demise. The poet does not mourn the "vile world" he will have left, but begs the youth to forget him, and to erase even the memory that he wrote these sonnets, lest reading them bring grief. This negative memorial urges the youth not even to utter the poet's name after his death because, on account of his association with the poet, he is likely to suffer social censure. The unambiguous statement at the end of the sestet, "for I love you so," encapsulates the tone of this sonnet. It is significant that the mortality sequence begins as soon as the poems have passed the number seventy, that is, "three score and ten," the biblically designated span of human life.

Sonnet 72

The reason that the beloved might suffer the mockery referred to in the last line of the previous sonnet is revealed here as the alleged unworthiness of his verse, and potentially whatever else his life has produced. As a result of the greater specificity about the source of his shame, the tone of this sonnet is even more self-deprecatory than the previous one. The poet begs the addressee not to lie about his merits when pressed to give an account of his life. As in the preceding sonnet, the poet calls for complete oblivion, urging that even his name should be forgotten, and in both poems this plea occurs in line 11.

Sonnet 73

Changing his perspective for that of the addressee, the poet considers the view of his increasing decrepitude from the perspective of the beloved. In this, one of the greatest of all the sonnets, the controlling metaphor is that of the poet's life compared to seasonal change and organic decay. Contemplating his demise in successive quatrains, the first quatrain compares the poet to a tree losing its leaves, the second to the end of day, the third to a fire extinguished in its own ashes. The line at the end of the first quatrain is one of the most famous in English literature, "Bare ruined choirs, where late the sweet birds sang." While its powerful simile implies no emotional ambiguity whatsoever, the line summons up a range of images, especially since choirs is spelt "quiers" in the Quarto: of singing, both the song of actual birds and potentially the choirs that sang in chancels and abbeys now razed to the ground since the desecration of monastic life, and the poet's own lyrics, his song, written on "quires" of paper. These leaves, whether paper or otherwise, connect the first quatrain with the departure and separation ("leave") of the last line. The final couplet acknowledges the fact that the youth knows the poet is dying, and that the imminence of his death intensifies his love for the poet.

Sonnet 74

In this, the last of the morality set beginning at 71, the poet now consoles the addressee, reasoning that "the better part of me," his spirit, belongs to the young man and will remain with him. Evoking the language of the marital bond of indivisible identity, the poet explains that while the dross of his life will indeed be lost, what is best and essential to it endures. This sonnet registers a shift in sentiment from the previous poems in which the poet has expressed shame about his life and work. Here, in contrast, he urges the youth to reread the poems as the part of himself that he consecrated to the youth.

Sonnet 75

The young man holds an almost eucharistic significance in the poet's life. He is the poet's feast and his treasure. The poet's desire for the youth takes on more secular connotations than those of the first two lines where the beloved figures as "food to life" and rain upon the earth, when at the end of the first quatrain Shakespeare returns to earlier images (from 47, 48, 52, and 56) of a miser "feasting" on his treasure. The sonnet thus rehearses the cycles of physical and emotional desire, which run the course from satiety to starvation.

Sonnet 76

Leaving the theme of mortality, the poet resumes that of the quality of his verse and the impossibility of its ever doing justice to its object. In particular, the poet apologizes for its lack of novelty, which is indeed stylistically the case – Shakespeare was not an innovator in the sonnet form. The reason for this monotony is that the object of his love, and therefore of his verse, does not change. Thus, the sonnets become a testament to the poet's emotional constancy.

Sonnet 77

While the mirror and the clock will register the march of time, "this book," a blank book that seems to accompany the poem by way of a gift, will receive the impression of the recipient's mind and allow him to commit to paper all that he will otherwise forget. Use of this book will impart self-knowledge.

Sonnet 78

In this, the first of the "rival poets" sonnets (78–80, 82–6), the speaker worries that others are now taking the young man as the object of their verse. The implication is both that they are writing about him and dedicating poems to him. Despite the intimacy between the speaker and the youth, the poet is now in competition for his patronage, thus the plea at the sonnet's conclusion that the youth is his only benefactor suggests a relation of economic as well as emotional dependency.

Sonnet 79

The first quatrain laments the loss of the poet's monopoly on the young man's patronage. Acknowledging that the young man deserves a better poet than himself, he claims that the rival is an unworthy one whose poetry is merely plagiarism, stealing beauty from the youth and claiming it as his own work. The gendered pronouns in this sonnet refer not to the addressee but to the rival (invariably male) poet.

Sonnet 80

Interestingly, the poet again defers to his rival's superior skill. The controlling image is that of seafaring, which while it derives from Petrarch takes on a very different tenor here, perhaps because of the defeat of the Spanish Armada in 1588, where the great Spanish navy fell prey to the agility and pluck of more humble English vessels. Although the rival's tall ships are ostensibly greater than the little boat, "the saucy bark" belonging to the poet requires a smaller investment from his patron, and thus a lesser risk. The worst that can happen is that the poet will be destroyed by his devotion to the youth.

Sonnet 81

In a brief hiatus from the theme of his rivals, the poet now considers whether the youth will predecease or survive him. Even if the poet does not live to write the youth's epitaph, his name will live forever in the sonnets. This is a classical topos, deriving most significantly from Ovid. Ironically, of course, it is Shakespeare's name that has endured whereas we do not know the identity of the nameless young man. That the poet expects to be interred in a "common grave" while he anticipates an elaborate funeral monument for the youth emphasizes once again the vast class differences between them.

Sonnet 82

The first line of this sonnet reproaches the youth for betraying his Muse even though he acknowledges (as he did, for example, in the servile Sonnet 57) that the young man is entitled to read anything he wishes. However, the youth gives his blessing indiscriminately, albeit that his thirst for knowledge causes him to seek for poetic novelty. Arguing for his own "plain words" as opposed to the elaborate artifice used by his rivals, the poet accuses them of merely daubing the young man's beauty with cosmetics. Thus, his beauty is actively impaired rather than enhanced by his rival's verse.

Sonnet 83

Continuing directly on the theme of "painting" or cosmeticizing, the poet disparages the second-rate poetry of his rivals. He likens their work to the lifeless replicas that represent the deceased on funeral monuments. Crucially, matter without spirit is the defining characteristic of bad art in the sonnets. There may have been, however, a certain prescience on Shakespeare's part in this judgment, because he himself acquired a profoundly inadequate funeral monument at the Holy Trinity Church in Stratford after his own death. Since the youth is alive, surely, claims the poet, he does not need the embellishments of funeral art.

Sonnet 84

In another bid to oust his rivals, in the final couplet the poet comes dangerously close to saying that the youth's susceptibility to flattery impairs his artistic taste and actually encourages the inferior verse, described in the body of the sonnet, that is being written on his behalf. This sonnet also continues the argument for plain style, here figured as the accurate copy of the young man, whose beauty and worth need neither ornament nor elaboration.

Sonnet 85

Reverting to the less critical account of his rival expressed in 79 and 80, the poet is reduced to mute illiteracy by the eloquence of his rivals. He asks only that the youth value him for his direct and outspoken utterance, even as he reads the work of the rivals. The irony here is, of course, that the "dumb" poet has composed a highly complex sonnet, whose eloquent rhythms flow by means of the echoing consonants that claim to be lost for words.

Sonnet 86

Returning to the naval imagery of Sonnet 80, the poet claims that it is not his rival's greater, supernaturally inspired, poetic prowess that has killed his own powers of poetic expression. Rather, it is the fact that the rival has not only dedicated his poetry to the youth but has also written poems about him, thus depriving the speaker of "matter," that is, the most fundamental substance or topic of his verse.

Copious quantities of critical ink have been spilt on trying to determine the identity of the rival poet referred to here. George Chapman is the foremost candidate on the grounds that he translated Homer's *Iliad* from the Greek, and thus learned his craft from the "spirits" of poets long dead. However, it is far more important to ascertain the qualities Shakespeare ascribes to the poet's rivals – his assessment of their art – rather than to determine their identities.

Sonnet 87

Implicitly because of the rival poet's superior claims on the youth's affections, the poet relinquishes all claims on his beloved patron. The poet assumes a posture of servile subjection, reasoning that he did not deserve the youth's admiration and devotion in the first place, bestowed only because at the time of the gift the youth did not know either his own worth or that of the poet. The youth's attentions have been as a dream from which the poet has had a rude awakening. The feminine rhymes in this sonnet may reflect his dependence on the youth.

Sonnet 88

In yet another expression of the idea that the poet and the beloved share a single identity because in their relationship the two have become one, the poet anticipates (as he has earlier in Sonnet 49) the moment of his rejection. At that time, he will take the young man's part against himself because his love is such that he is willing to bear all injury.

Sonnet 89

The poet continues in his condition of masochistic abjection, claiming that if the youth hates him, he must hate himself.

Sonnet 90

The poet pleads that if the youth is to desert him, he should do it with a clean break. Already beset by woes, it would be better if the youth left him now before his misfortunes increase because then he will know the worst loss he could experience, by comparison with which other ills will be easier to bear.

Sonnet 91

There is no material pleasure that can surpass the happiness the poet takes in his friend. Further, his connection with the friend brings worldlier honor than expensive clothes or aristocratic pastimes. His only fear is that if the youth spurns him, he will then have lost everything.

Sonnet 92

Directly connected with the conclusion of the preceding sonnet, even if the young man does abandon the poet, it will not matter because that will kill him. This makes the poet invulnerable to abandonment, secure as he is in the knowledge that he will not have to endure life while deprived of the friend's love. The couplet, however, reintroduces a note of vulnerability, namely that the poet may simply not know that the fair friend has already betrayed him.

Sonnet 93

Again deploying the image of the bond between the poet and the fair friend as a marital one, the speaker imagines living like a betrayed husband, unaware that he has been betrayed. The poet grounds his suspicions in that the friend's beauty prevents any trace of his ill-deeds being registered there, and returns to the image of the dichotomy between the mind and heart, but here the division is within the youth, not within the poet. The friend's features may leave no trace of his heart's infidelity.

Sonnet 94

The poet's suspicions now unfold by way of a generalized proposition, the complex interplay between outward appearance and inner truth. This disparity between the inner and the outer has complex facets, so that it is laudable when those who look powerful or dangerous behave in ways that are contrary to their demeanor. On the other hand, those who look beautiful but who are inwardly treacherous are worse than those whose despicable appearance at least represents what they are without deception.

Sonnet 95

Probing again this disparity between beautiful appearance and morally flawed – or even depraved – character, this sonnet pursues the images of the cankered rose, of diseased beauty, whose infections and stench have been opposed to beauty and perfumed fragrance in preceding sonnets (for instance, Sonnet 54). Whereas the previous sonnet examined these issues in general, almost philosophical, terms, this sonnet confronts the youth directly with his sexual notoriety.

Sonnet 96

In a direct narrative continuation of the previous sonnets, the poet assesses contrasting views of the friend's moral defects, which are either condemned as delinquency or excused as high spirits. The poet excuses the youth's error once more. Like jewels on a queen, even the least expensive is still valuable. However, at the Petrarchan turn, the poet takes a much harsher tone, comparing the youth's crimes with those of the proverbial wolf in sheep's clothing. The final quatrain pleads with the youth not to mislead his admirers or the poet with his beauty, his prodigious capacity for deception.

Sonnet 97

Sonnets 97–100 treat a separation between the poet and the friend, whose absence in this poem is like winter to the poet, even though it is summer and autumn, that is, the period from the summer equinox, June 21, to September 22. The fruits of autumn are reminiscent of a posthumous birth.

Sonnet 98

Here the poet is absent from the fair friend in the spring. As personifications analogous to the poet and the friend, youthful April and the astrological figure of aged Saturn play together. The poet, however, bereft at the absence of his friend, can take no pleasure in such sport nor in the advent of summer and its flowers because they are merely shadows of the greater, but absent, beauty of the young man.

Sonnet 99

This uniquely fifteen-line sonnet shares certain thematic resonances with the rival poet sequence, which accused other poets of theft, or conversely, enjoined them to copy the youth without embellishing what they saw. Still in the summer, and, as the poet promised in the preceding sonnet, playing with the shadows of the friend, the poet accuses nature's blossoms of plagiarism, of stealing the friend's beauty. One red and white flower has stolen from both aspects of the friend's beauty, and would also have taken his breath, were it not that a canker (a figure also used in 35.4 and 95.2) killed him.

Sonnet 100

A new sub-sequence begins here in this sonnet addressed to the poet's Muse who has been neglecting the fair friend in favor of other subjects. The relationship between the poet and the friend seems to have returned to a greater and less troubled state. Enjoining her to redeem the time thus wasted in "gentle numbers," or new poems, the poet asks the Muse to look again at the beloved's face, and if there are any wrinkles she is to write in condemnation of time, or else to lend "my love" fame faster than time can destroy him.

Sonnet 101

In a second sonnet addressed to his Muse, the poet reasons that no doubt she is silent because the youth is so beautiful, and his beauty so intermixed with truth that he needs neither adornment nor praise. Thus continues the poet's critique of garish and inept art. The poet, however, makes the case that the Muse has it in her power to immortalize the youth. In the concluding couplet, the poet takes the role of preceptor, showing the Muse how this is done, and thus appropriating her office as his own. Even though the addressee of this sonnet is the usually feminine Muse of poetry, the gender is not specified, perhaps because in Sonnet 38 the poet claimed the fair friend for his Muse.

Sonnet 102

This sonnet continues to refer to a period of silence on the part of the poet, which been the controlling paradox since Sonnet 100. The speaker claims that though he writes less, his love for the friend has in fact intensified, and he again refers to the danger of "publishing" the beloved as a form of crass merchandizing. This was also the theme of Sonnet 21 and was the reason Lucrece was raped by Tarquin in *The Rape of Lucrece*. The poet's former productivity was early in their relationship, and he likens his poetic "song" to the traditional lyrical image of the nightingale, Philomel, who sings only at the onset of summer. The relationship between the youth and the poet is as worthy of song as it ever was, but the poet refrains lest he weary the youth with repetition.

Sonnet 103

As in Sonnets 3 and 77, the poet enjoins his friend to look into his mirror. In this sonnet, he is to look there for compensation for the fact that the poet is allegedly unable to write on account of his uncooperative Muse. The poet's lines would only try to embellish what is already perfect (the cardinal sin he has criticized in other versifiers).

Sonnet 104

The poet refers here to the addressee as "fair friend." Clearly, time has passed, three years, since they first met. This period of time is arguably autobiographical, but it is also something of a lyrical convention, appearing in the classical poet Horace as well as in Shakespeare's contemporary Samuel Daniel and the work of French Renaissance poets. The speaker reassures the friend that he will never age in his eyes, even though his eyes may be deceived. He tells future generations of readers that beauty died long before they were born, with his friend.

Sonnet 105

The friend is now referred to as "my beloved," and the poet's devotion to him is so great that he is wary of charges of idolatry. The language the poet uses to exculpate himself from this charge, however, is entirely religious, and the poem's repetitions read like an incantation. Claiming that he is a monotheist because he worships only the young man, the poet details the youth's trinity of virtues in a way that courts blasphemy.

Sonnet 106

Although this has been one of the sonnets usually moved by critics who have claimed that the order in the 1609 Quarto does not reflect Shakespeare's intention, in fact, this sonnet continues the idea of love as a religion announced in the previous sonnet. In this secular rendition, previous descriptions of beauty are posited as merely prophetic anticipations of the young man's beauty, which heralded the youth in a way that is analogous to the Old Testament prophets who foresaw the coming of Christ. Previous generations lacked sufficient capacity to sing his praises because they had never seen the youth, whereas now people who see his beauty are simply dumbstruck by it.

Sonnet 107

The biographer of the Earl of Southampton, G. P. V. Akrigg, claims that this sonnet was addressed to the Earl on his release from the Tower of

London because it opens celebrating the emancipation of the beloved from what had seemed like the inevitability of death, "a confined doom." Intriguing though this interpretation is, there is, as with all aspects of biographical speculation concerning the sonnets, no evidence for it, though there are heavy suggestions of topical allusion. The sonnet does indeed seem to refer to a particular moment, to an improvement in the wider social world, not just in nature or in the poet's relationship with the young man. The beginning of the second quatrain has also been understood as a metaphor for the death of Elizabeth, "The mortal moon," because she was associated with Diana, the goddess of chastity, whose emblem was the moon. The moon has passed, peace has come, and even Death knowing that the poet will be immortalized in these poems is compelled to torment peoples who are without language. Again, the latter may be an allusion to the "tribes" of the New World that the English were beginning to encounter. This is one of the most confident and unqualified assertions of the immortality of verse in the Quarto.

Sonnet 108

If the goal of the poet's art is that of accurately depicting himself and the beloved, what is left to him but repetition once he has accomplished that goal? This is the aesthetic dilemma confronted by 108, as Shakespeare reaches the number of sonnets that comprised Sidney's *Astrophil and Stella*. Picking up again the Petrarchan idea of love as a religion, the speaker declares, using a direct echo of the Lord's Prayer, "hallowed thy fair name," that he must repeat his praises like prayers. The most repetitious prayers were those associated with banished Catholicism, the rosary. The aesthetic goal, like the goal of such prayers, is to infuse fresh feeling with each iteration.

Sonnet 109

The poet begs the addressee never to accuse him of infidelity even though he has been "absent," that is, either physically apart from or otherwise distant from the beloved. He could no more leave the beloved than leave himself, and he returns at the promised time with (in a decidedly religious image) water to wash away his offense. Although the poet is subject to the usual range of human weaknesses, he would never betray his love, "my rose," "my all."

Sonnet 110

Like several sonnets in the Quarto, this one begins with a dramatic and direct declaration to the addressee. In what seems to be the continuation of an exchange begun in the previous sonnet, which sought to allay the beloved's insecurities, this sonnet begins with a confession that he has "wandered," with the implication of both journeying and straying from fidelity to the young man. The opening lines are often taken to be a reference to Shakespeare's traveling as an actor whereby he has made himself "a motley to the view." He claims that these deviations from his devotion to the beloved have in fact served only to intensify it by comparison. Promising never more to "grind" his (implicitly sexual) appetite elsewhere, he now begs to be taken back by the beloved.

Sonnet 111

The argument between the poet and the young man continues as the former apologizes for the means by which his fortunes compel him to earn a "public" living, unlike the addressee whose status seems to obviate the necessity of earning money. The allusion appears to be to the public stage, and to Shakespeare's relationship to his own art in the famous lines: "Thence comes it that my name receives a brand, / And almost thence my nature is subdued / To what it works in, like the dyers hand" (6–7). Just as the dyer's hand is indelibly stained by what it works in (especially in this era of woad-based dyes), so are the poet's name and identity branded by his craft. "Hand" is a synecdochal reference to writing, and the poet's hand is potentially stained by ink, the medium in which he works, while his character is tainted and defaced by the environment in which he "for my life provide[s]" (line 3). Significantly, Shakespeare draws an analogy between the writer's profession and artisanal labor, rather than with some more exalted sphere of activity. This far from illustrious account of the poet's vocation comports with the moral condemnation of the theatre that was widespread in the period. Indeed, there are suggestions of base criminality in the "brand" that is inscribed on his body as the mark of his profession. Felons too were branded with a hot iron for their misdeeds, and some of them were close acquaintances of Shakespeare's, like fellow poet and playwright Ben Jonson, who was branded on the thumb with an "M" for murderer after he killed another actor in a brawl. In another religious metaphor, one again associated with the Catholic practice of confession, the poet begs the youth to give him a "penance" and begs for his pity as a cure for his tainted condition.

Sonnet 112

The poet has been subject to some sort of public disgrace – perhaps merely the dishonorable profession of the stage alluded to in the previous sonnet. Here it is not, as in the previous sonnet, merely his hand that is marked by his labor, but in an intensification of the image of being marked by what one has done, the image is now one of being branded on the forehead like a criminal. However, heedless of the opinions of others, he cares only for the young man's estimation of him. Biographical critics have read line 4, "o'er green," as a reference to Robert Greene's attack on Shakespeare as an arrogant "shakes-scene."

Sonnet 113

Absent again from the fair friend, the poet sees only the image of the beloved in everything he sees, an idea explored in Sonnet 53, and in the sense that the youth constitutes the beloved's universe (see also, for example, Sonnets 109 and 112). This sonnet offers a philosophical meditation on how emotion shapes both physical vision and the capacity for discernment or moral judgment, the uncertainty about which is voiced in the concluding line.

Sonnet 114

Continuing on the theme of perception, especially the doubts that crept in about the veracity of his vision at the end of the preceding sonnet, the poet's skepticism is expressed via the image of a king who is susceptible to flattery. The speaker's eye may be deceived, and thus he is deluded into transforming evil into the image of good. Drinking poison that appeared benign, then, is an honest mistake. The greater evil is the initial attraction to the sight of a poisoned cup.

Sonnet 115

Returning now to the theme of time, the poet explores the paradox that even the most ardent and sincere declaration of love does not account for how love grows over time. Thus the poet's previous declarations have been "lies," exactly what poetry was accused of being by those Puritan elements in Shakespeare's society who thought it ungodly. Time may prevent the fullest expression of love, but for all that, since love is in its infancy, it would be a lie to say, "now I love you best." This sonnet suggests that the love between the poet and the youth has been renewed, and that love is again as fresh as in its first stages.

Sonnet 116

This is arguably the most famous and widely quoted of the sonnets because of its confident assertion of the constancy of love despite mutability and change. The language used here echoes that of the marriage service, in which the congregation are asked to voice their knowledge of "impediments" to the marriage. The poem draws out the distinction between love that is subject to time, change, and death and love that is not, claiming that only the latter deserves the title of love. The concluding proof of the argument is made in specifically legal language, although recent criticism has (erroneously) tried to ambiguate what is meant to be a legally sound assertion.

Sonnet 117

The dialog between the poet and the friend continues as the speaker confronts, as in the preceding sonnet, in specifically legal terms, the accusation that he has been negligent in his attentions toward the young man. Although he admits to having spent time with other lesser minds and has been guilty of "willfulness and errors," he pleads that his intention was only to test the young man's commitment to him.

Sonnet 118

This sonnet explores the idea that desire is a physical appetite, subject to satiety and craving variety, while love is a malady whose cure may be as bad as the disease he has contracted, which in this instance seems indubitably venereal.

The poet's defense against the youth's accusations despite the admission of infidelity continues in this poem, but now in terms of dietary and medical similes, particularly the metaphor of purging, the practice of taking emetics to induce vomiting. Seeking the variety represented by bitter food and medicine in order to sharpen his appetite for the youth and to regain his health, the poet has sought out the company of those who offer a marked contrast to the young man as a way of anticipating and preventing discord, "illness," in their relationship. There are implications of promiscuity and venereal disease and the unpleasant remedies it necessitates. The poet has learned his lesson, and the couplet plays on two senses of disease: first, that the poet became bored with the young man, and secondly, that the poet's love for the young man was itself a disease.

Sonnet 119

The now ailing poet contemplates his infidelity to the young man, implicitly in the image of "Siren tears," with a woman who has lured him into danger. Finding that just as ill-tasting medicine improves health, love restored is love increased, which means that despite his unpleasant experiences, the poet has gained more than he has lost.

Sonnet 120

Consoled by the fact that the youth once betrayed him (Sonnets 33–5, 37–8), the speaker claims the youth must offer the same balm of forgiveness that the poet then offered him. In the tit-for-tat account of their mutual infidelities, the poet nonetheless conveys the agonies both of remorse and of betrayal.

Sonnet 121

Having acknowledged transgression in the previous sonnets, the poet now bridles against the reputation he has gained for promiscuity. Now going on the defensive, the speaker argues that those who spread such rumors are merely projecting their own corrupt natures.

Sonnet 122

Following on from the image of "reckoning up" abuses in Sonnet 120, this poem rejects the notion of keeping count in love relationships, which is somewhat ironic if read in view of the preceding sonnet in which the poet seems to think he has evened up the score of infidelities.

The youth had given the poet a table book containing his own writing (potentially the blank notebook the poet gave him in Sonnet 77, urging him to write in it), and the youth is now aggrieved that the poet has not kept it as a cherished gift but has given it away. The speaker defends this act, claiming that he needs no record of the book because its contents are emblazoned in his memory. Thus, keeping the book, the poet reasons, would be a sign that he had forgotten the young man.

Sonnet 123

Perhaps written in response to the newly erected monuments to celebrate the accession of James I to the English throne in 1603, the addressee of this poem is not the young man but time, to whom he issues a defiant statement that his love will endure despite change. However, the argument of the preceding sonnet continues that material objects and historical records have their value completely distorted by time's "continual haste."

Sonnet 124

This sonnet again puts the relationship between the speaker and the young man in the perspective of the public world. The reader is thus at a much greater distance than the face-to-face (or face-to-mirror) proximity and intimacy that the majority of the sonnets convey. Love, the poet contends, is not subject to the vagaries of time and political change.

Sonnet 125

The poet responds here to the wider world of status, flattery, politics, and pomp. Condemning those who live for such superficial and transient honors, particularly the "suborned informer" (most likely time himself) of line 13, he argues the virtues of simplicity. This movement away from direct address to the young man again provides some perspective and distance on a relationship that by and large we are shown up close. In this, the third consecutive sonnet in which the poet contends his love is not subject to change, he criticizes the world of status and privilege in a way that also suggests his exclusion from it.

Sonnet 126

Two lines short of the customary fourteen, this lyric is composed of six rhymed couplets and in the first line contains the famous reference to the addressee as "my lovely boy." It is an *envoy* or farewell to the young man, placed as it is at the end of the series of poems addressed primarily to him. It recapitulates the major themes of the sonnets that have gone before, namely the fundamentally aesthetic problem of preserving beauty despite the depredations of time. While the sonnet begins by claiming that the "boy" has time within his grasp, the poem ends with a threat, namely that nature, so proud of her workmanship in creating the youth, can only delay and not halt the aging process whereby he must be surrendered to death.

Sonnet 127

Marking the division in the Quarto between the sonnets addressed to a man and those addressed to a woman, this first sonnet in the so-called "dark lady" section nonetheless takes up issues which were central to the first 126 poems, namely the nature of beauty and the relationship between beauty and art, specifically cosmetics, but implicitly alluding also to the kind of enhancements the rival poets were in the habit of deploying.

While blackness was hitherto understood to be the antithesis of beauty, black is now the new "fair." A light complexion is no longer beautiful because it is subject to disgraceful and deceptive cosmetic enhancement. The poet's mistress has eyes so black that they seem to mourn those who counterfeit their beauty with cosmetics, and in this they are so alluring that, paradoxically, they become the epitome of beauty. While this argument, a mock encomium, or poem of praise, cleverly reverses the Petrarchan convention of the fair lady, it also plays upon it: Stella's eyes are black.

Sonnet 128

The unorthodox beauty of the mistress having been established in the first sonnet of this series, the poet goes on not only to praise her skill as a musician but also, in a well-worn conceit whereby the lover envies the proximity between the lover and an intimate object, to wish to change places with the keys on her instrument. The poet imagines the woman entertaining the keys as lovers who impudently kiss her fingers as she tickles, or erotically stimulates, them.

Sonnet 129

The speaker seems to have achieved the sexual proximity he admired and envied in other "jacks" in the previous sonnet. While even engaged in the ostensibly innocuous playing of the virginals in the previous sonnet involved the image of a woman with many lovers, this sonnet takes the tone of bitter and arguably misogynist disgust at having consummated their relationship. The first line of this sonnet, "Th'expense of spirit in a waste of shame," is probably the most compact expression of repugnance at ejaculation in the English language. It is also the only sonnet devoid of both possessive adjectives and personal pronouns.

Sonnet 130

This sonnet is in the anti-Petrarchan tradition, that is, a tradition that reverses the traditional conceit of the beautiful, blonde, virtuous, and incidentally unattainable woman. In light of the sonnet that precedes it, the poet's mistress is all too attainable. Going through the litany of Petrarchan metaphors, the poet declares his love as beautiful as any woman ever described with such hyperbole. The deeply ambiguous final line adds humor to the game of reversal.

Sonnet 131

The poet's mistress may not look like the paragon of Petrarchan beauty, but she certainly behaves like one, being every bit as tyrannical and cruel as the best of them. Others have said that this woman is not attractive enough to provoke the lovers' torments that the poet endures on her account, but it is, he avers, not the case. Further, her black beauty is fair with him, and it is not her physical appearance that troubles him but her black deeds.

Sonnet 132

Returning to the idea expressed in Sonnet 127 that the woman's black eyes are mourners, that is, sad, expressive dark eyes, the poet claims they pity the pain she has inflicted upon him. Again exploiting the eye/heart dichotomy that was used in the young man series, the poet begs her heart to be as merciful as her eyes.

Sonnet 133

This sonnet treats the love triangle between the woman, the youth, and the poet. It accuses the woman of "engrossing," that is, taking and mistreating the young man as well as himself. The poet is now bereft of the woman and the youth, and even, since the latter is his "next self," of himself as well. Since she imprisons him, the cruel woman has everything that belongs to the speaker, including, of course, the young man.

Sonnet 134

Picking up on the language of "engrossing," that is, the illegal practice of greedily hoarding, especially grain, and thus creating scarcity, this sonnet uses contractual legal and financial terms to argue for the release of the youth into the poet's custody.

Sonnet 135

This and the sonnet following make a pair of poems that pun on the word "will." Though it long predates Freud, the poem is an unequivocal answer to the question, "What does a woman want?" The poet's answer is bawdy obscenity in a game of verbal ingenuity about the woman's alleged voracity as well as her vast sexual orifice in which he will "hide" his "will" (line 6), the equivalent of "willy" in modern British slang. There are no fewer than thirteen references to "will" and one to "wilt." Interestingly, these poems probably offer most evidence that contradicts the popular view that Shakespeare's sonnets are harmlessly "romantic."

Sonnet 136

The speaker argues that among so many lovers, one more will not make a difference. The punning on "will" continues, and the assertion in the final line that "my name is Will" is often taken as evidence that the sonnets are indeed autobiographical.

Sonnet 137

In a much more serious tone of emotional engagement, addressed to Cupid, the poet accuses him of having tampered with his vision so that he has been enthralled by a woman who has neither external beauty nor inner moral qualities. Once again, the sonnet plays up the distinction between the eye and the heart and the capacity of desire to delude the judgment.

Sonnet 138

Again, striking a poignant emotional note about the nature of sexual intimacy, in contrast to the mutual distrust explored in the young man sonnets, this sonnet describes a relationship that is grounded in mutual self-deception: she swears her fidelity to him and he pretends to believe her in order to offer a false presentation of himself as youthfully naïve. The sonnet is replete with puns (known in rhetoric as paronomasia) and double meanings, the most significant of which is "lie," to sleep with and to deceive.

Sonnet 139

This sonnet begins in the throes of an argument in which the woman will no longer speak to or look at the speaker. In a direct address to the woman who appears to have asked the poet to justify his behavior, the poet ostensibly gives her total power over him as in the Petrarchan tradition. He begs her to attack him verbally rather than by withdrawing. He says that he can bear it if she loves other men, so long as she does not cast her gaze at them while with him. In order to salve these wounds, he persuades himself that since her looks have hurt him before, she now averts her gaze so as to slay others and not wound him again. He begs that she return her killing looks on him so that he can be put out of his misery.

Sonnet 140

The torment of the poet's relationship with the woman continues. Fearing madness, the poet implores her to declare that she loves him.

Sonnet 141

This sonnet explores the idea of love as a compulsion that cannot be accounted for even by those qualities that men find to love in women. His desire for the woman far exceeds any appeal she might have to his sensual appetite. Enslaved by the woman, the poet declares that he does not love her with his senses, but only with his heart. The reference to plague as an appropriate punishment for the sin of loving this mistress has occurred earlier in relation to the woman in Sonnet 137.14. This image of disease may imply here, as it does in that sonnet, that the pain the speaker experiences is not only emotional but also that of venereal disease.

The eye/heart opposition also appears in Sonnets 24, 46–7, 93, and 132–3.

Sonnet 142

Both the poet and his mistress have committed abundant sexual transgressions. Since that is the case, the poet claims that she has no right to reprove him for his promiscuity. He pleads with her to develop a sense of pity so that pity may be shown to her, otherwise it may be refused to her by her own example.

Sonnet 143

In this, the third and last instance in which the word "Will" figures prominently and apparently as an onomastic pun, the first octave consists of an extended simile in which a housewife (the mistress) runs after an escaped barnyard fowl (her other lover or lovers), leaving her infant (the poet) in sore distress. In a merry chase, the woman pursues the bird taking flight, while the wailing babe chases his mother. The poet hopes that the woman will turn back and love him like a mother. This is an extraordinary and unique image of the lover as dependent infant whose grief and loss magnify the poet's emotional distress.

Sonnet 144

One of the most famous of the sonnets, Sonnet 144 addresses the love triangle that is also the subject of Sonnets 40–2 and 133–4. The man "right fair" may be one and the same as the fleeing fowl of the preceding sonnet. The first line appears to be a straightforward assertion of the poet's bisexuality. The love triangle is imaged as the medieval psychomachia in which the good and evil angels battle for the man's soul. In the sonnet's reconfiguration of the psychomachia, however, instead of vying for possession of the young man's soul the evil angel tries to turn the good one, in a way that registers the linguistic proximity between the two, from "friend" to "fiend." That is, the woman is tempting the man into sexual congress with her, and the poet is tormented by this suspicion because he cannot verify it.

Sonnet 145

On an entirely different register of both emotional intensity and lyrical sophistication, this sonnet is believed on grounds of the pun it contains on "hate away" to have been one of Shakespeare's earliest poems and written about his wife, Anne Hathaway. Composed in octosyllabic lines, it is stylistically unique.

The woman has said that she hates the speaker, but seeing how this distresses him, she recants.

Sonnet 146

This is a reflection on the classical theme of *vitae summa brevis*, the brief span of life, though couched in Christian terms. There is no addressee here but the poet's own soul as he contemplates aging and death.

Sonnet 147

We return to the feverish love the poet feels for his mistress, and to the image of loving her literally (rather than metaphorically) as a disease. He is obsessively attached to the woman, even though she is what precipitated his madness and caused his reason to desert him. That he is indeed mad is proved by his complete misperception of reality, having taken the evil woman to be, contrary to empirical evidence, fair and bright.

Sonnet 148

Continuing directly from the end of the preceding sonnet, the poet contemplates how his judgment and vision could have become thus distorted.

Sonnet 149

In the previous "will" sonnets the poet was fully in control of his faculties, but now, blinded by love, the poet is incapable of doing other than his mistress's bidding. In fact, he has so far lost the capacity for independence of will that he even masochistically punishes himself when she is angry with him.

The sonnet begins in the middle of yet another argument with the mistress in which she has charged that he does not love her. The speaker asks how this could be possible when he even takes her part against himself, shuns those she spurns, and berates himself for incurring her displeasure. She commands; he worships. For all that, he urges her to continue to hate him because now he knows that she "loves"/seduces all who can see, and he is blind – and thus, by implication, exempt.

Sonnet 150

The poet attempts to fathom the woman's emotional power over him. The claim that others abhor the woman would seem to undermine the persuasiveness of his case that she should love him more because of it.

Sonnet 151

In an extended pun on penile erection, this sonnet asserts the triumph of physical desire over soul and conscience.

Sonnet 152

In this sonnet, the poet seems to indicate the fact that his mistress, more than being simply promiscuous, is married to someone else, "thy bed-vow broke" (line 3).

Sonnet 153

The conceit of this sonnet, and the one that follows and concludes the Quarto, for all that it derives from a six-line epigram in the *Greek Anthology* by Marianus Scholasticus, a poet of fifth-century Byzantium, is nonetheless about venereal disease. In the *Greek Anthology* version of the story, napping Cupid entrusts his torch or flaming brand to the nymphs, who see the opportunity to rid the world of lust by extinguishing it in water. However, the torch burns with such ferocity that it lights even water, making the cold water hot. In Shakespeare's version, it is the poet's mistress who reignites Cupid's quenched flame, leaving the speaker to seek a cure in hot water, which was in fact a treatment for venereal disease. The bath, however, has no power to heal him; only the mistress's eyes can do that.

Sonnet 154

The last sonnet reiterates the story, but with some variation. On this occasion, the napping Cupid again has his torch pilfered by a maid of the goddess of chastity. Consecrated virginity thus defeats desire. The votress extinguishes the flame in a well, causing it to become a hot pool and a remedy for various ailments. Taking the bath, the speaker discovers that while the flame of desire heats water, water cannot cool love. The Quarto concludes, then, with the poet still in love but also diseased and in torment.

Notes

Preface

1 References to Ovid's *Metamorphoses* are from *Ovid's Metamorphoses, The Arthur Golding Translation 1567*, edited with an introduction and notes by John Frederick Nims, and with a new essay, "Shakespeare's Ovid," by Jonathan Bate (Philadelphia: Paul Dry Books, 2000). References to Ovid's *Amores* and *Ars Amatoria* are taken from *Ovid: The Erotic Poems*, trans. Peter Green (Harmondsworth: Penguin, 1982); those to Petrarch's *Canzoniere* are from Mark Musa's translation (Bloomington: Indiana University Press, 1996). With the exception of references to *Romeo and Juliet*, which are taken from my own *Romeo and Juliet: A Contextual Edition* (Boston: Bedford Books, 2003), all references to Shakespeare are taken from *The Norton Shakespeare*, ed. Stephen Greenblatt (New York: W. W. Norton, 1997).

Chapter 2   Identity

1 Even though Geoffrey Chaucer had appropriated Petrarch's Sonnet 132 for the *Canticus Troili* in *Troilus and Cresseide*, the imitation of Petrarch's great poetic achievement in English did not begin in earnest until early in the sixteenth century.
2 *TLS*, October 2, 1937, p. 715; October 9, 1937, p. 735.
3 See appendix, Sonnet 86.

Chapter 3   Beauty

1 In the 1609 Quarto, hues is spelt *"Hews"* and, like *"Rose,"* is capitalized and italicized. It has been taken by some readers as a coded reference to the

fact that the fair young man must have been called Hugh (a first name) or Hughes (a surname).

2 Sir Walter Ralegh, "Nature, that washed her hands in milk," Harleian MS 6917; Edmund Spenser, *Amoretti* (1595), Sonnet 64.

Chapter 5 Numbers

1 Katherine Duncan-Jones, among others, has argued that there is also numerological significance to the numbers of the sonnets themselves. Most strikingly, minus the first seventeen procreation sonnets, and Sonnet 126, which is not properly a sonnet because it has only twelve lines, there are 108 devoted to the young man, exactly the same number of sonnets as are contained in Sidney's sequence, *Astrophil and Stella*, a length much imitated by his associates (Duncan-Jones, 1997, 97–101).

2 On the importance of Petrarchan rhetoric in *Romeo and Juliet*, see Dubrow, 263–7.

3 M. T. Clanchy, *From Memory to Written Record: England 1066–1307*, 2nd ed. (Oxford: Blackwell, 1993), 124.

4 My thinking on this sonnet is indebted to Katheryn M. Giglio's brilliant discussion of Jack Cade's reference to the score and tally in *Henry VI*, Part 2, "Unlettered Culture: The Idea of Illiteracy in Early Modern Writing" (unpublished dissertation, Syracuse University, 2006).

5 For a full discussion of this topic, see Norman Jones, *God and the Money-lenders: Usury and the Law in Early Modern England* (Oxford: Blackwell, 1989).

6 For a detailed analysis of this phenomenon, see Peter Herman's excellent essay in Schiffer.

7 Katherine M. Wilson, 262, argues that Shakespeare's sonnet is a direct parody of Sidney.

Chapter 6 Time

1 Kerrigan, 34.

2 Park Honan, *Shakespeare: A Life* (Oxford: Oxford University Press, 1998), 172.

Works Cited

Akrigg, G. P. V., *Shakespeare and the Earl of Southampton* (Cambridge, MA: Harvard University Press, 1968).

Baker, J. H., *An Introduction to English Legal History*, 4th ed. (Oxford: Oxford University Press, 2002).

Bate, Jonathan, *The Genius of Shakespeare* (London: Picador, 1997).

Blakemore Evan, G., ed., *The Sonnets* (Cambridge: Cambridge University Press, 1996).

Booth, Stephen, *An Essay on Shakespeare's Sonnets* (New Haven: Yale University Press, 1971).

Booth, Stephen, ed., *Shakespeare's Sonnets* (New Haven: Yale University Press, 1977).

Burnett, Mark Thornton, ed., *Christopher Marlowe: The Complete Poems* (London: J. M. Dent, 2000).

Burrow, Colin, ed., *The Oxford Shakespeare Complete Sonnets and Poems* (Oxford: Oxford University Press, 2002).

De Grazia, Margreta, "The Scandal of Shakespeare's Sonnets," in Schiffer, 89–112.

Dubrow, Heather, *Captive Victors: Shakespeare's Sonnets and Narrative Poems* (Ithaca: Cornell University Press, 1987).

Duncan-Jones, Katherine, *Shakespeare's Sonnets* (Arden edition, London: Alan Nelson, 1997).

Duncan-Jones, Katherine, *Ungentle Shakespeare: Scenes from his Life* (London: Arden, 2001).

Erne, Lukas, *Shakespeare as a Literary Dramatist* (Cambridge: Cambridge University Press, 2003).

Gascoigne, George, *The Pleasauntest Workes of George Gasgoigne Esquire: Newlye Compyled into one Volume* (London, 1587).

Graves, Michael A. R., *The Tudor Parliaments: Crown, Lords and Commons, 1485–1603* (London: Longman, 1985).

Greenblatt, Stephen, *Will in the World: How Shakespeare Became Shakespeare* (New York: Norton, 2004).

Gurr, Andrew, "Shakespeare's First Poem: Sonnet 145," *Essays in Criticism*, 21 (1971), 221–6.

Herman, P. C., "What's the Use? or, The Problematic of Economy in Shakespeare's Procreation Sonnets," in Schiffer.

Hotson, Lesley, *Mr. W. H.* (New York: Alfred Knopf, 1965).

Hotson, Lesley, *Shakespeare by Hilliard* (Berkeley: University of California Press, 1977).

Kerrigan, John, *The Sonnets; and A Lover's Complaint* (New York: Penguin Books, 1986).

Kyle, Chris R., "'But a New Button to an Old Coat': The Enactment of the Statute of Monopolies, 21 James I cap. 3," *Journal of Legal History*, 19, 3 (1998), 203–23.

Peterson, Douglas, *The English Lyric From Wyatt to Donne* (Princeton: Princeton University Press, 1967).

Phillips, Adam, *On Flirtation* (Cambridge, MA: Harvard University Press, 1996).

Roberts, Sasha, *Reading Shakespeare's Poems in Early Modern England* (New York: Palgrave, 2003).

Rollins, Hyder Edward, *A New Variorum Edition of Shakespeare: The Sonnets*, 2 vols. (Philadelphia: J. B. Lippincott, 1944).

Schiffer, James, ed., *Shakespeare's Sonnets: Critical Essays* (New York: Garland, 2000).

Schoenfeldt, Michael, "The Matter of Inwardness: Shakespeare's Sonnets," in Schiffer, 305–24.

Schoenbaum, Samuel, *Shakespeare's Lives*, new edition (New York: Oxford University Press, 1993).

Steele, Timothy, *Missing Measures, Modern Poetry and the Revolt Against Meter* (Fayetteville, AR: University of Arkansas Press, 1990).

Vendler, Helen, *The Art of Shakespeare's Sonnets* (Cambridge, MA: Harvard University Press, 1999).

Waller, Gary, *English Poetry of the Sixteenth Century* (New York: Longman, 1986).

Welty, Eudora, *One Writer's Beginnings* (Cambridge, MA: Harvard University Press, 1984).

Whitworth, Charles, ed., *The Comedy of Errors* (Oxford: Oxford University Press, 2002).

Wilde, Oscar, *Portrait of Mr. W. H.: A Problem of the Sonnets* (Greenwich, CT: Literary Collection Press, 1905).

Wilson, J. Dover, *The Sonnets* (Cambridge: Cambridge University Press, 1967).

Wilson, Katherine M., *Shakespeare's Sugared Sonnets* (New York: Barnes and Noble, 1974).

Wood, Michael, *Shakespeare* (New York: Basic Books, 2003).

Wright, George T., *Shakespeare's Metrical Art* (Berkeley: University of California Press, 1988).

Index